D0386788

"Unless we ask questions, we don't get answers. Antipas Harris, without hesitation or trepidation, has not only realistically and learnedly dealt with the quintessential 'elephant in the room' looming in the minds of many black millennials, but he has expanded our vision and understanding of Jesus Christ, the Bible, and cultural relevancy. I love his acknowledgment of the problem and his clarity in rendering a biblical solution. This is indeed good news for all of God's children!"

Dale C. Bronner, founder and senior pastor of Word of Faith Family Worship Cathedral, Atlanta

"Antipas L. Harris has produced a pivotal and timely work. He boldly probes the question that few have dared to address, Is Christianity the white man's religion? Harris shows that Christianity and the Bible promote justice and ethnic relevance for all people. The nature in which our current faith reading lenses need historical correction vis-à-vis our propensity toward westernized acculturation and racialized hermeneutics is critical in our attempts at reconciliation and effective ecclesiology. Harris deserves applause for further addressing an important matter with depth and clarity."

Jamal-Dominique Hopkins, dean of Dickerson-Green Theological Seminary and associate professor of biblical languages and literature at Allen University

"*Is Christianity the White Man's Religion?* sensitively touches some of the most inflammatory and diversely viewed areas of the Bible. It invites readers to explore their own sensibilities and motives and come to their own conclusions. Dr. Harris has definitely jumped into the ocean of divide with both feet, and this book will definitely make waves. . . . He has presented this controversial topic with truth, tact, and sensitivity. I wholeheartedly recommend this book to anyone who wants to share the gospel of Jesus Christ without prejudice, and I sincerely hope that all Christians of all cultures get a copy and begin a journey that so many have refused to take. Antipas L. Harris asks the question, Is Christianity the white man's religion? Read this book and I'm sure you'll find the answer."

John Francis, founder and pastor of Ruach City Church

"Many folks look at Christianity and conclude it is not for 'people like us.' Antipas digs down to the roots of Christianity before history and culture began to interpret it. He has created a resource that centralizes the Bible and helps connect Christian faith in light of lived injustice. This book is a gift for those who are seeking authentic spirituality but feeling dissonance between their spiritual hunger and how Christianity is being lived out."

Nikki Toyama-Szeto, executive director of Evangelicals for Social Action/The Sider Center

"Dr. Antipas Harris courageously confronts the academic view and spiritual ramifications of a debate that has existed in the black community and beyond for years! The lack of understanding is limiting our ability to represent the body of Christ. This book's genius is that every person concerned about how our world has become so polarized will see that the roots are in part wrapped around the misrepresentation of religious rhetoric—sometimes innocently conveyed—and how it's had its hand in the historical cookie jar! At the end of the day, we who are spiritual must take the lead on becoming one, which is our responsibility. . . . Jesus prayed that we might be one! Enjoy the read!"

Bishop T. D. Jakes Sr., senior pastor of The Potter's House of Dallas

"In this very timely and provocative book, practical theologian Antipas Harris revisits the age-old question of Christianity's relevance for people of color. Given the resurgence of certain strands of white supremacist iterations of Christianity and the attendant political and ethnic polarization that results, *Is Christianity the White Man's Religion?* seeks to offer the church a way forward. Adding his voice to the chorus of voices that are struggling to keep American Christianity from losing its soul, Harris deserves a reading by students, ministerial practitioners, and engaged citizens."

Eric Williams, curator of religion at the Smithsonian National Museum of African American History and Culture

IS CHRISTIANITY
THE WHITE MAN'S
RELIGION?

HOW THE BIBLE IS
GOOD NEWS FOR
PEOPLE OF COLOR

ANTIPAS L. HARRIS

An imprint of InterVarsity Press
Downers Grove, Illinois

InterVarsity Press
P.O. Box 1400, Downers Grove, IL 60515-1426
ivpress.com
email@ivpress.com

©2020 by Antipas Lewis Harris

All rights reserved. No part of this book may be reproduced in any form without written permission from
InterVarsity Press.

InterVarsity Press® is the book-publishing division of InterVarsity Christian Fellowship/USA®, a movement
of students and faculty active on campus at hundreds of universities, colleges, and schools of nursing in the
United States of America, and a member movement of the International Fellowship of Evangelical Students.
For information about local and regional activities, visit intervarsity.org.

All Scripture quotations, unless otherwise indicated, are taken from The Holy Bible, New International
Version®, NIV®. Copyright © 1973, 1978, 1984, 2011 by Biblica, Inc.™ Used by permission of Zondervan.
All rights reserved worldwide. www.zondervan.com. The "NIV" and "New International Version" are
trademarks registered in the United States Patent and Trademark Office by Biblica, Inc.™

While any stories in this book are true, some names and identifying information may have been changed to
protect the privacy of individuals.

Cover design and image composite: David Fassett
Interior design: Daniel van Loon
Images: cropped female hand: © Ling Luo / EyeEm / Getty Images; cardstock texture: © Zakharova_Natalia
    / iStock / Getty Images Plus; light wood texture: © t_trifonoff / iStock / Getty Images Plus; blank
    postage stamp: © troyek / E+ / Getty Images; watercolor background: © Sergey Ryumin / Moment
    Collection / Getty Images; gold foil texture: © Katsumi Murouchi / Moment Collection / Getty
    Images; abstract background: © oxygen / Moment Collection / Getty Images; abstract oil painting: ©
    photominus / iStock / Getty Images Plus; two hands typing: © Emma Innocenti / Digital Vision /
    Getty Images; Afro American female hand: © LightFieldStudios / iStock / Getty Images Plus; Holy
    Bible with cover glow: © boonchai wedmakakawand / Moment Collection / Getty Images; Mosaic of
    Jesus Christ: © Lilly3 / iStock / Getty Images Plus; hand: © Hanis / E+ / Getty Images; abstract
    watercolor: © lutavia / iStock / Getty Images Plus; tree illustration: © izumikobayashi / iStock /
    Getty Images Plus; blue watercolor: © licccka / iStock / Getty Images Plus; Bible: © DNY59 / iStock /
    Getty Images Plus

ISBN 978-0-8308-4599-6 (print)
ISBN 978-0-8308-4825-6 (digital)

Printed in the United States of America ♾

InterVarsity Press is committed to ecological stewardship and to the conservation of natural resources in all our
operations. This book was printed using sustainably sourced paper.

Library of Congress Cataloging-in-Publication Data
A catalog record for this book is available from the Library of Congress.

P	21	20	19	18	17	16	15	14	13	12	11	10	9	8	7	6	5	4	3	2	1
Y	37	36	35	34	33	32	31	30	29	28	27	26	25	24	23	22	21	20

DEDICATION

I would like to dedicate this book to

*Jakes Divinity School, where we are forming people of faith
for innovative leadership in the church and society;*

*the furtherance of rigorous knowledge and deep spirituality,
for the purpose of defending the faith and bearing
witness in the public square;*

the global yearning for reconciliation;

and all those who wonder whether God cares about them.

CONTENTS

PART ONE

THE CHURCH AND THREATENING CONTEMPORARY IDEAS

CHAPTER ONE

THE STRIKING QUESTION

Race in America is a form of religious faith, and we will
never be able to understand or address it with the necessary
knowledge, energy or commitment until we comprehend its true
architecture. . . . How might we overturn this racial architecture
that is built inside Christian life and practice in the West?

WILLIE JENNINGS

I was teaching a graduate course on ministry leadership when a twenty-two-year-old student interrupted my lecture with a bizarre question: "What do you say to your friends who are leaving the church and arguing that Christianity is the white man's religion?"

I was taken aback by the question. First, it was unrelated to the topic of the day. Second, I wondered who in the world would argue such a thing.

The class discussion that ensued opened up a world of discovery. I couldn't shake the conversation out of my mind for several weeks. Since then, I've learned that many young people of color across North America, all over Europe, and throughout Africa are often wary of Christianity because of current religious alignments with divisive politics, not to mention the global history of pain already associated with branches of Christianity. Many Christians (like I was) are unaware of the current conversations about this on the streets. My concern and subsequent research led me to write this book.

The question of whether Christianity is a trustworthy religion for everyone is not new. Over the years, many people and groups have asked this question. For example, the Nation of Islam was convinced that Christianity was the white man's religion, dating back to the Jim Crow era of racial segregation. It is deeply concerning that since then, after all the changes that have taken place, this question has resurfaced. A new wave of religious skeptics has arrived with serious questions about faith, identity, and the struggles of everyday life. From followers of the Nation of Islam and the Five Percent Nation to students of Science and Consciousness and others, there is a circumspection regarding oppressive attitudes and beliefs associated with the history of Western Christian practice. Times have changed, but similar observations that provoked the question years ago are provoking skepticism today.

The student's question brought to mind three distinct situations, one of which occurred in 2002 when I was a student at Yale Divinity School. Just outside the barbershop on Dixwell Avenue in New Haven, Connecticut, a group of self-identified black, Jewish men sold kosher hot dogs. One day, one of them stopped me and asked who I was, where I was from, and what I did. My interest in theological studies caught his attention. He felt the need to share with me that black people are the true Jews. To be honest, the conversation was rather intriguing; it was my first encounter with an African American who claimed to have found his true identity. His serious and intelligent conversation kept my attention for longer than I intended. Before this point, my only point of reference to black Jews was Ethiopian Jews. It was clear, however, that the brother in New Haven was not talking about the Jews who are native to Ethiopia. He was saying that African Americans are Israelites and don't know it.

Several years later, I was invited to speak on urban evangelism for the Solid Rock Church Conference at the Founder's Inn in Virginia Beach. A pastor from Washington, DC, expressed concern about a group of African Americans who seemed to connect well with the young black men in Washington's distressed areas. He explained that these men wore yarmulkes, called themselves Israelites, and sought to convince other young men that Christianity is the white man's religion and that black people are the true Israelites. It was an earful! Immediately, I made the connection with the "black Israelite" I had previously met in New Haven.

In 2011, I went with a group of college students to New York for an Urban Plunge Excursion. We partnered with the New York School of Urban Ministry (NYSUM). Students interested in urban evangelism joined us on 125th Street to pray with passersby. Energized by the pedestrians' openness to spontaneous prayer, some of the students wandered a bit further down 125th Street to a bus stop near the Apollo Theater. *More people to pray with*, they thought.

From a distance I noticed that a few of the students were having a lively conversation, so I went to join them. As I approached, I realized that the young seminarians were in an intense theological conversation with brothers from the Nation of Islam. With a quick-talking New York style, the Nation of Islam brothers were trying to persuade our slower-talking Virginian seminarians that Christianity is the white man's religion.

The brothers from the Nation of Islam were quite versed in the tenets of their own faith as well as Christian Scripture. However, I noticed how they misquoted the Scriptures to suit their own agenda. While I do not remember the specific passage, I recall inserting myself into the conversation and calling them out on the misquotation. I then abruptly invited my students to return to the rest of our colleagues on the other end of the street. As I left the brothers from the Nation of Islam, I remember thinking, "Our students have got to know the Scriptures!"

In 2017, Bishop T. D. Jakes shared with me that he was planning to host a Global Think Tank on the African seedbed of Christianity at that year's International Pastors and Leadership Conference.

Ironically, the conversation with the bishop was only a few days after my seminary student shared his concern about the growing skepticism that many urban youth and young adults have about Christianity.

I soon learned that pastors all over the Western world are concerned about the foothold the Black Hebrew Israelite movement and other religious groups are gaining in urban areas. Eight thousand pastors and leaders gathered at Bishop Jake's global think tank that addressed the African presence in the Bible. They wanted tools to prepare their congregations to defend the faith in everyday conversations, such as around dinner tables, on street corners, and in barber shops and beauty salons.

As a whole, millennials are more educated than previous generations. The combination of the "more educated" and "undereducated" creates a tension of knowledge in society and raises a lot of questions. Some of those questions are about religion. In an internet age where information is rampant, it is hard to distinguish valid information from what is invalid. People are getting information from everywhere. Much of it is laced with uninformed opinions. We are often caught in a maze of uncertainty, trying to determine what is trustworthy.

For this generation, religion must touch the heart and not simply mandate rules. Touching the heart goes beyond cozy emotions and speaks to practical dynamics of faith. In other words, genuine religion touches the streets. It champions causes and advocates for justice. It helps people gain a moral compass, discover their identity, and develop gifts—which is exactly what my family and church provided for me at a young age.

GROWING UP IN THE BLACK, SANCTIFIED CHURCH

I grew up in a small Pentecostal church in Manchester, Georgia. Pentecostal churches were often called "sanctified churches" because they placed a heavy emphasis on "living holy." While the sanctified church emphasized personal piety, it also drew on Scripture to cultivate our moral conscience, illuminate our personal identity, and strengthen us in our gifts. My dad and mom started our church in the early 1970s, and most of our members were African American. My formative years of faith were rooted and grounded in my experience with God.

Our church was a place of refuge, encouragement, and empowerment. We had a community made up of everyone from single-parent families to two-parent families with tons of children. My parents had eight kids and another couple had fourteen. We were like one big family who loved God and each other. Church was everything for us. We worshiped up to four times a week. Our faith taught us that Jesus understands our social and personal situations—a truth that became so deeply rooted in our faith orientation that, for us, Jesus was black like us. Don't get me wrong—our church did not preach that Jesus is African American. What I mean is that when we read the Bible, we interpreted Jesus through the lens of our experience.

For black people, blackness is more than a color. It is a rich heritage, a contribution to the world. For blacks with a history of slavery, to be black involves a history of pain and social struggle. Black Christian history, the one that framed the origins of black churches, passed down a grassroots understanding that Jesus loves us amid a hateful world. Jesus journeys with us through life's ups and downs. He is with us when down in the dumps just like God was with Israel during their time in Egypt. Just as God imputed identity to Israel and made a people of them, our identity was formed in Christ. We are "Jesus people." For centuries, millions of black people have relied heavily on that identity. More than two hundred years of slavery and almost a century of Jim Crow honed a common faith in black churches that our hope must be in God. We have believed that he would make a way when none was visible. And in our little church in Manchester we witnessed the Lord do just that, time after time.

We experienced God as a father for the fatherless, a mother for the motherless, a friend for the friendless, water for the thirsty, and food for the hungry. Jesus sided with us amid pain, frustration, agony, and loss. The redeeming Christ saved us from sin. The crucified Christ acquainted himself with black suffering. The loving God would help us succeed against all odds. Again and again, my life story confirmed such a God!

My dad even established a school at our church. It was a place to deepen our faith through a Christian education curriculum, provided an escape from youthful vices, and helped the children of the church navigate the contours of southern racism. Even in the 1990s, the black experience in the Deep South was tough, but for most of my young life I didn't realize it. When I discovered the reality of racism, I was shocked out of my mind!

We had very friendly relationships with white Pentecostal congregations. We visited their churches, and they came to ours. But there were nagging reminders that the two churches were different. Partly, the black orientation to church differed from the way white people experienced church in the Deep South. For example, one time our church took a youth group to a skating rink in Griffin, Georgia, because it was the closest location to Manchester with a weekly Christian music skate night. While at the skating rink, my dad (our pastor) and a white pastor developed a friendship. Each week, they would chat about the faith, church life, and vision for their ministries. At one Christian skate night, the white pastor told my dad that a black man was coming to his church, but he didn't really know how to relate to him. So he suggested that the man come to our church. Never mind the distance from Griffin to Manchester is about forty miles, which is an hour drive time.

Conversely, our church's focus on helping black people succeed in Christ was not always an inviting experience for white people. For example, during one of my dad's practical sermons on the necessity of personal responsibility, he paused and asked the congregation a question something like, "Why does God want us to be responsible and work?" Forgetting that we had a white visitor that day, a brother in the church responded, "So we can pay these white folks their money!" Only after he spoke did he remember the visitor and quickly say, "Oh, excuse me!" Many of us laughed, including the visitor, but this story illustrates how our faith was formed within a context of the black experience against a dominate white society that we viewed as indifferent to black people.

One traditional feature of African American churches was that they helped blacks synthesize their faith within the broader context of white economic and ideological superiority. The way we learned about God, Jesus, and the Bible helped us succeed in the white world. However, in a predominately white society, most white people can't relate to being in a situation where they are the minority. Most could probably live their lives without ever experiencing a majority black context.

Black churches in the Deep South not only constituted a majority of black people, they also preserved some of the qualities passed down from the slave and Jim Crow era religious traditions. This is probably the case because there was really no theological or liturgical model to which to subscribe; it was just the way black people did church. Their spirituality was inextricably formed alongside their experience. Princeton religion professor Albert J. Raboteau points out, "The slaves' historical identity as a unique people was peculiarly their own. In the spirituals the slaves affirmed and reaffirmed that identity religiously as they suffered and celebrated their journey from slavery to freedom." One must not dismiss cultural identity too quickly. African American spirituality was formed through the pressures of oppression. Black human and Christian identity were shaped in spite of a society that rejected both. Black families and churches safeguarded young minds and lives from mainstream identity adversity.

THE SHADOW OF JIM CROW

I was blessed with parents and grandparents who, in some ways, continued the historic African American approach to childrearing.

Although nearly a hundred years had passed since the abolition of slavery, my grandparents grew up in Georgia during Jim Crow's segregation. My parents caught the tail end of it as well. The attitudes that permeated Jim Crow and the structural systems set in place from the nation's inception, in many ways, continue until this day. So my parents invested a lot of time and support in my siblings and me. At the time, I did not realize how much they shielded us from the ugly experiences they had endured.

Now that I am an adult, some of the funny but serious experiences they shared from their life under the Jim Crow era's segregation come to mind. For example, Dad went to a restaurant when he was a teenager. After walking through the door, the owner, a grumpy white man, said, "We don't serve n———s." Dad said that he humorously responded, "Oh, good; I don't want one of those. I want a burger," then took off running for fear the man would try to hurt or even kill him. In the Deep South, in those days, it was not always clear who were members of the Ku Klux Klan (KKK)!

Black churches were very helpful in navigating a society in which we lived, but felt powerless to change. In addition to family and nurture, black churches gave my brothers and me a platform to express our musical talent and preaching. Our singing group, the A Boys (later renamed A7), went from church to church, singing and proclaiming the gospel. Our intense involvement in church shielded us from much of the lingering racial problems of the Deep South. They made us feel important, loved, and affirmed. Who could lose with that kind of support?

Reflecting on it, though, I have mixed emotions. On the one hand, it was helpful that my parents safeguarded us and that our church provided a refuge from racism. It helped that my faith was grounded in the black church at an early age. I often wonder what life would be like if I didn't have the foundation that I had. By the time I was exposed to society's original sin, my faith was strong in the God I had met long before.

On the other hand, it was hard to find my own voice. Even worse, I struggle with second-guessing my ideas. When one holds back from sharing their perspective, society is cheated of their contribution to human progress. For me, second-guessing traces back to my childhood. So many young people of color suppress their ideas for fear of societal contempt.

Dr. Martin Luther King Jr. encouraged blacks to be leaders. I think this is one of the reasons I love his messages so much. King said, "A genuine leader is not a searcher for consensus, but a molder of consensus." King lived leadership that molded consensus. However, his outspokenness resulted in his assassination. Black parents who remember his murder face a moral dilemma in child-rearing: Do they want their children to live? Or do they want them to speak their minds? King would be an anomaly if he were the only example. But the corridors of history are decorated with heroes who spoke up for justice and lost their lives as a result of it.

In spite of the exemplary work of our forefathers and foremothers who gave their lives for the freedoms we enjoy, many people continue to live with the same quandary: Should I speak up or keep silent? Should I act or refrain from doing anything at all? Should I stand boldly or acquiesce?

Certainly, everyone can relate to this point. Every human being confronts a similar moral dilemma. Many people experience loss simply because they speak up for truth, are rejected for sharing their stories, and are excluded for pointing out problems that adversely affect society. At best, many have learned to go along to get along because if they fight back, they might not live to tell.

COLLEGE DAYS

Growing up in Manchester, racial problems in my little hometown paled in comparison to some other southern towns. I never met anyone wearing white sheets and hoods. For most of my early life, I thought I had never met a member of the KKK. However, when

I was a student at LaGrange College, I spent a lot of time in the community and became friends with a white classmate who grew up in LaGrange. He knew a lot about the town, and he knew a lot of the people. One day, he shared with me that someone we knew from the community was part of the KKK. She was actually one of their leaders who led local gatherings, which were then non-violent—as far as we knew. When my friend told me this, it freaked me out! Had I lived in a bubble all this time? I was under no illusion that everything was hunky-dory with regard to race relations, but I was swiftly learning that I was not that far removed from racist history. In fact, it may have been more dangerous because the lines of separation were not as clear as they were under Jim Crow.

Another time during college, my brother and I decided to branch out and fellowship with white Pentecostal churches. Although we were raised in a majority black church and an all-black parochial school, we had adjusted quickly to a majority white college. I preached at a special service one Sunday night at a white Pentecostal church in LaGrange. It was packed with young black and white people, mostly from the college. Since the church had been dwindling in attendance, the pastor was particularly excited to see so many young people that night, so he asked my brother and me for a meeting to discuss joining his staff. At the interview, the first question he asked was, "What do you all think about interracial marriage?" Shocked by the question, we said, "We have no problem with it." The pastor openly expressed concern that if we were to join his staff, we might fall in love with one of the white women in his church. He then explained, "I would be concerned about those poor children. They would not know if they are white or black." Needless to say, our working relationship with that church did not materialize. Confused and feeling rejected, I struggled to grasp why the anointing on my life could not overcome my blackness.

One may question my reasons for bringing up my college days in this book. Some would say that times have changed, and this story is anachronistic. But let's not jump to conclusions so quickly! If Trayvon Martin, Michael Brown, Eric Garner, Sandra Bland, Aiyana Stanley-Jones, Mya Hall, Jemel Roberson, Botham Jean, Atatiana Jefferson, and others could come back to life, they would argue otherwise. They are dead. There is just no convincing rationale for their deaths. Surprisingly the courts did not even convict their assassins! Could it be that their blackness posed a threat to public safety? When black and white Christian leaders don't work together to address such public concerns, young people tend to make sweeping conclusions that Christianity remains part of the race problem.

While I hope society finally moves beyond the race problem, we must not deny that the problem remains a reality. I have been followed in stores and overlooked for opportunities for which I was more qualified than the person(s) hired. On two separate occasions, my brothers and I have stopped at gas stations to fill up and grab a snack only to be stopped by a white cashier who told us, "All y'all can't come in here at the same time." Because we were black, we were criminal suspects upon arrival. When I share this experience with my white friends, they are appalled. Groups of white men enter stores all the time and never have this kind of experience.

It is all the more heartbreaking when negative attitudes against other people are either embodied or perpetuated by people who claim to be Christians. When I discovered this, I was dumbfounded. I had come to know Jesus as one who loves everybody. Why in the world don't his people do the same?

DEMANDING A NEW FAITH

These days, young people are searching for meaning and identity. While the church was the context of my youth, nowadays young people do not experience church the same way. Research is showing that they are enthralled with spirituality more than ever but are rejecting the church.

One of my professors at Boston University, the late Dale Andrews, once pointed out, "Black urban youth and the black middle class feel that church has become irrelevant to their daily struggles. At the core of their frustrations lie displaced faith identity conflicts." Churches in black communities are important symbols of faith and places where black people congregate for certain events such as weddings, funerals, and so on. However, the traditional, dominant cultural assumptions about the faith are no longer hallmarks of black Christianity like they were as recently as the '80s and '90s. There are many reasons for this, among them technological advancements with global influences and the influx of new ideas and shifts in family structures. The internet has replaced both the textbook and the library. And far fewer parents are requiring their children to go to Sunday school or church at all. Fewer and fewer youth and middle class people see places with steeples as spaces of self-discovery and spiritual formation. They take their questions to the bookstores, classrooms, and internet. Google is the new card catalog, opinions are the new source of knowledge, and online video portals such as YouTube and Netflix are the new pulpit. So, while people are more spiritual today than previous generations, what they see in the media and online shapes their vision of the world, God, and themselves.

A growing number of youth and young adults are opting for subcultural identity groups (i.e., gangs) and alternative religious groups such as science and consciousness groups, five percenters, the Nation of Islam, Black Israelites, Wiccans, and varying forms of witchcraft to guide them in self-discovery and their search for success. Similar to my early orientation to the Christian faith, spirituality in these groups tends to be experience based. Experience must not be underestimated, but it is varied and complex. It can be very difficult to find one's self without a sound faith foundation.

Difficult times, broken dreams, family misfortunes, and broken hearts will send one's life into a tailspin of doubt and even atheism. However, even the most cynical person wonders if there might be something out there somewhere to help cope with life.

Pew Research reports that millennials are reluctant about going to church and don't value Scripture as a guide for living. Yet they are more spiritual than previous generations. For millennials, spirituality is the search for a God who cares about their everyday life and is concerned for the flourishing of their lives.

One wonders if the church's interpretation of Scripture has not kept up with the questions of this generation. Meanwhile, alternative spiritual groups are offering responses to this generation's questions and an increased number of both college students and career-focused urban millennials are buying what they are teaching. While these religions have profound differences, they commonly emphasize the integration of spirituality into everyday life, and their ideas have infiltrated contemporary hip hop, pop, rock, and country music; literature; and poetry.

We must revisit the roots of Christianity, reckon with its decorated history, and advance a renewed vision of the faith.

I am deeply concerned that Christianity—with such rich gifts of unity, love, and hope at its foundation—is losing its meaningfulness in American cities. We must revisit the roots of Christianity, reckon with its decorated history, and advance a renewed vision of the faith. That way, we can restore the integrity of Scripture and unveil the necessity of the church such that this generation and future generations will better connect with the church.

I have spent a lot of time thinking about the question my student asked me about Christianity being the white man's religion. Since then, the issue has come up again and again in conversations with other millennials. So, I spent some time with an interdisciplinary group of scholar-friends, some of whom participated in helping me during the writing of this book. I have come to the conclusion that the question of Christianity being the white man's religion is not merely an attack on Christianity. Neither is it meant to insult white people or attack white men. It is an honest question of contemporary relevance of the faith in a diverse world.

The question challenges a history in which groups of professing Christians have used the Bible in ways that oppress others. It rejects systems that claim Christianity as foundational while privileging some and creating underprivileged situations for others. Demographic predictions observe a significant increase of ethnic diversity in American cities. Amid this change, the question of Christianity being a white man's religion expresses concern about pervasive white male ideology in society's structures. Many young people believe that the Bible and Christianity are responsible for the oppression, hate, and destruction of identity such ideological superstructures have caused.

LIVING IT OUT

A brief housekeeping note: At the end of most chapters, you will find a section like this one labeled "Living It Out." My goal is to keep this book practical and provide readers with a quick summary and application of what they've encountered in the chapter.

As one seeking to understand the relationship between faith and contemporary culture, I have observed that millennials who question the relevance of the Bible and the church tend to do so in light of their lived reality. In a complex world of brokenness, people are looking for a faith that gives them meaning and a reason to hope again. Unfortunately, contemporary expressions of evangelical Christianity provide little of what this generation needs. This is especially the case with black, urban millennials. I was in a deep conversation with a former drug pusher who asserted, "Doc, you've got to take the religion to the streets!" His point was that right now there is a chasm between the Bible and the people in the streets. There is a gap between what local churches sometimes care about and what the majority of people need. Millennials are often turned off with "church" and they reject the Bible. For them, Christianity is the religion of the oppressors and the Bible does not affirm blacks, other minorities, or women in their pain and suffering.

A closer look at the Bible and a renewed focus on love, compassion, and justice will refresh us with living water to quench our never-ending thirst for spirituality and social justice.

Churches like the one from my childhood are few and far between. Or maybe churches like that are simply ineffective in today's social climate. There are certainly far less close-knit families such as the one I am privileged to have. As a result, the way we do church and the focus of the Christian message must respond to the changing times. However, Christian leaders tend to promote a faith that arguably supports systems of oppression and blames the downcast for their plight, overlooking the pain in the streets. The affirmation of ethnic diversity in the message of faith, and the practice of faith in social advocacy and policymaking, are necessary to meet the needs of today. A lack of attention given to these dynamics in contemporary society lends to the question that continues to resurface: "Is Christianity the white man's religion?"

I will further unpack challenges of faith in a generation in which black and brown millennials, post-millennials, and Generation Z are searching for identity and a sense of belonging. Something is happening that has created a loss of trust in the faith. I want to rediscover biblical Christianity for a better grip on what the Bible is really about and the hope that the faith offers.

For example, learning a bit more about ethnic diversity in Scripture helps young people of color better identify with the faith. I never cease to be amazed at how people's ears perk up when I talk about the black presence in the Bible. Time and time again, they are surprised to learn that there are people of color in the Bible. For some traditional Christians this is a trivial fact, and perhaps that is the problem. A generation in search of connection with the Ultimate Being requires more information about God than they are getting from traditional Christianity. I worry that the richness of hope, love, compassion, and acceptance in Christ escapes a faithless generation through the shadows of perceived oppression. To excavate Scripture and the essence of biblical Christianity sheds light on a far more inclusive than exclusive Christ, more empowering than disempowering, and more affirming than demeaning faith. This says to the contemporary unbeliever that, contrary to popular belief, biblical Christianity is God's gift to those who struggle with a sense of identity and belonging, social injustice, and oppression. A closer look at the Bible and a renewed focus on love, compassion, and justice will refresh us with the living water to quench our never-ending thirst for spirituality and social justice.

CHAPTER TWO

A CRISIS OF FAITH

Christianity in our age, in our moment, has functioned in and as, shall we say, the midwife of the production of social misery.

J. KAMERON CARTER

The Western world is facing a crisis of faith. In the United States, there is a decline in church attendance and an uptick in religious skepticism. At the same time, from classrooms to the streets, people are grappling with similar questions that people have always had about faith, God, and the Bible. They are interested in spirituality, social justice, personal significance, and how to live a good life. Studies show that millennials are reading more than any other adult generation. But they are not reading the Bible! The church and the Bible are no longer where they look for answers. The crisis of faith is probably more dire than many Christians realize. According to a 2019 Pew Research survey, "65% of American adults describe themselves as Christians when asked about their religion, down 12 percentage points over the past decade." Church is quickly becoming more of a symbol of conflict, oppression, and hypocrisy. Christian history is filled with supporting evidence to validate the suspicion. From American slavery to the Holocaust in Germany to South African apartheid, the powerful have leveraged the Christian faith for their own greed and political interests. Christ's message is often entangled with agendas that privilege some people and disadvantage others.

MILLENNIALS AND CHURCH

Research shows that more and more millennials have negative opinions about the church. At the Public Religion Research Institute, Robert P. Jones and Daniel Cox conducted a study on millennials' attitudes about the church using Middle Collegiate Church in New York as a case study. They found that young people see the church as exclusionary and even judgmental of people who don't believe in everything they believe. Many are leaving the church, and the ones who remain don't attend worship regularly.

African Americans remain more likely than whites to attend church. However, the Pew Research Center reports an uptick in religious disengagement among black youth and young adults as well. Peter Beinart, associate professor of journalism and political science at City University of New York, reports that African Americans under the age of thirty are three times as likely to avoid church affiliation as African Americans over fifty. The choice not to go to church is not only a preference but also a reflection of the shift in values. Recently an African American millennial explained to me that she left church because they were too closed-minded. She said, "I think church should be more inclusive."

Research bears witness that her position is not an anomaly. According to Jones and Cox, those who go to church are often ashamed to let their friends know they are Christians because Christians have a reputation of being narrow-minded:

> When I tell people I go to church, it's like a hassle. I have to couch it in all of these [qualifications]: "but it's very liberal," and, "Oh, Jewish people go there too, and it's young and old, black and white, and it's very diverse." I have to come up with

all these different ways of describing it. I have a little speech
... and I have to talk for way too long explaining this.

The decline in church attendance is already alarming. It is even
more disturbing that young Christians are embarrassed to admit
that they are believers.

Studies show that millennials are hesitant to admit that they are
Christians because they feel ill-equipped to handle questions about
Christian beliefs pertaining to human sexuality, female repro-
ductive rights, and more. In fact, most Christians are not equipped
to respond to the difficult questions without assigning political
preferences more than responding with the language of God's love.
Time and time again the Bible has been used to uphold sociopolitical agendas. As a result, people have suffered abuse in God's
name. Young people tend to view Christianity as small minded and
focused more on its institutional base than on economic empowerment, human rights, women's rights, the environment, and other
needs in the world. The world needs a spiritual awakening that
attends to personal and communal life.

The First Great Awakening of the 1730s and 1740s, the Second
Great Awakening of the 1800s, and the 1906 Azusa Street Revival
made indelible impressions on the global religious and spiritual landscape. There is a need for a new revival to reframe religious life in the
Western world. I believe that the next significant move of God will
be a spirituality that enlightens people's hearts and simultaneously
leads in the path of love that transforms the social strata of injustice.

Passing out tracts is no longer as effective a form of evangelism as
it once was. It is more important to listen and learn what people feel
they need. Also, the gift of listening is crucial when discipling others.
Listening will help the church develop better strategies to re-envision
the faith altogether. Top-down approaches will strangle the future of
faith. Listening draws in perspectives that are often overlooked and
aids in the development of more compassionate ministries.

The Barna Group conducted research in 2014 among eighteen to thirty-year-olds, and their discovery is deeply concerning. Only 32 percent of millennials read the Bible, including those who still claim to be Christians. Twenty-nine percent of millennials are happy to see other Christians reading their Bible in public. Only 10 percent of them engage in Bible study, while 21 percent say they are now atheists or agnostics.

The study also reveals that 15 percent of millennials have decreased Bible usage in a year's time. And the number of young Bible skeptics are now more than double the amount of older adult students of the Bible. Thirty-two percent of millennial skeptics say they feel the Bible is a dangerous and oppressive book.

WHERE ARE MILLENNIALS GOING?

Social justice–minded young people are faced with many options. I will mention two of them here. The first is devastating—to abandon Christianity altogether. And the research shows that this is already happening at alarming rates.

Luna Malbroux, an African American millennial blogger and former Christian, offers criticism that is insightful though difficult to hear:

> Steadily, it seems like when we move away from the Christian church, we move towards less organized spiritual practices based on traditional African spirituality. There have been no knocks on the door, no pamphlets, no billboards, no late-night hotlines, no viral video campaigns. And yet, an unnamed spiritual movement reimagining African tradition and nature-centered spirituality has been growing among young black Americans.

In Malbroux's view, some of them are leaving the church and are attracted to spiritualities that put them in touch with nature. Ironically, the Bible does not begin with religious institutions, creeds, and billboards. Nature is central to the biblical narrative and salvation story.

Genesis chapters 1 through 3 begin the Bible with a nature-centered spiritual environment in which God communed with humanity. Also, in the Gospels, Jesus died for the sins of the world. But salvation was not achieved in a synagogue or the Temple. Jesus confronted and accepted his fate in the garden of Gethsemane. The last thing the savior carried was not a Bible or an offering plate. He carried a tree trunk up a hill. His funeral was in Golgotha, where he hung on a tree in an open field. Perhaps many in this generation can benefit from another approach to biblical interpretation, an issue that I will take up in the next section of the book.

Another example of millennials leaving the church is DeShawn Tatem, also known as the Golden Child, from Hampton Roads, Virginia. Tatem was raised in the hood, though he went to church as a young child. His neighborhood was ravaged by prostitution, drug transactions, fights, shootings, and more. He participated in gang life until one day while standing at an ATM, a woman approached him and shared the love of Christ. He later surrendered his life to Jesus while watching Christian television. Golden Child then set out to share the love of Christ with others.

A rapper and pianist, the young evangelist was licensed to preach in 2007. He was determined to "go where the church would not go." He wanted to provide answers for young people in detention centers, jails, clubs, and rough neighborhoods, all of which Tatem referred to as "the gutta most"—a term describing the ghettos as the "uttermost part of the earth" (Acts 1:8 KJV).

According to the *Virginian-Pilot*, Tatem was once a member of New Covenant Outreach Ministries, a nondenominational church in Norfolk. However, he soon parted ways with traditional Christianity, claiming that his intellectual curiosity coupled with a passion to take spirituality to the streets was not satisfied within the traditional church. He grew more and more frustrated with what he saw as systemic injustice and the uptick of violence in his Virginian hometown. Tatem's spiritual quest led him to a conviction that

African Americans are really Black Hebrew Israelites. He moved to North Carolina and founded Yahshua The Movement, where he became known as "The General." According to reports, thirty-nine-year-old Tatem was shot and killed in Concord, North Carolina, at the end of November 2017. He was in a heated altercation with his organization's landlord when the landlord's girlfriend shot him.

I did not know Tatem, but we had mutual friends who fondly remember him as a very passionate and gifted man, one whose life was cut short far too soon. America's cities are filled with people like Tatem who are passionately desirous of a relationship with the God who affirms their identity, fights against injustice, cares for the broken, and adds tangible value to their human existence. There are millions of young people who are desperate for deeper spirituality and want to know more about God.

This was obvious to me in a thank you note I received from a young African American woman after the 2017 Global Think Tank on the African Presence in the Bible at Bishop T. D. Jakes's International Pastors and Leadership Conference in Dallas. The woman explained that over the past few years she had developed deep concerns about several of her close friends who abandoned their belief in Jesus. They became convinced that Christians are following the "white man's religion and the white man's Bible." The Think Tank extrapolated the positive black presence in the Bible and in early Christian history, which was an insight the young woman explained that she appreciated because much of the information gleaned from the urban streets is that the "white man's Bible" presents blacks as a cursed people. Prior to the Think Tank, the young woman didn't feel prepared to respond to the new, growing Christian challenge in urban America.

The second option for social justice–minded millennials is to seek creative ways to bridge the gap between faith and problems. To do so, they have to distance themselves from mainstream Christianity. People such as millennial pastor of Hillsong Church in

New York, Carl Lentz, said that he, like many young Christians, hesitates to identify as an evangelical Christian. He believes that associating with mainstream evangelicalism could hurt his global, urban Christian witness. He explained in an interview on MSNBC that he, in essence, is not "that kind of Christian," one who promotes confessional faith at the expense of hurting people. This goes to show that a generation of social justice–oriented young people, including young, social justice–minded pastors, are frustrated with the obvious injustice in our world. Some of them question the necessity of faith when it is used to create the problems or when it is silent about human suffering.

One example is the national spotlight placed on police killings of more than two-hundred-and-fifty black men and women between 2016 and 2019. Many of them were unarmed. Others such as Philando Castile in Minneapolis and Atatiana Jefferson in Fort Worth exercised their right to bear arms. They were both licensed to carry, just like millions of other Americans. In a society where the Constitution grants the right to bear arms, why was the police's blink response to shoot them? Youth of color believe that their blackness is more of a threat than weapons.

This belief is compounded with other situations in which unarmed, black youth were also killed, and justice in their cases continues to dangle in the balance. After George Zimmerman was acquitted of killing Trayvon Martin, scores of black, white, and brown youth led protests in major cities of America, chanting "black lives matter!" Similar events occurred when policer officer Darren Wilson was acquitted in the shooting death of Michael Brown. Young people are also leading the #neveragain movement to address school shootings and violent crimes in urban streets.

Shortly after the shooting of Michael Brown in Ferguson, Missouri, Yale Divinity School hosted a conversation with DeRay McKesson, who was one of the original members of the Black Lives Matter movement. McKesson expressed concern that churches hesitated to speak out for black bodies being killed in the streets. With a rather gentle critique of the church, he asserted, "Jesus would not have taken so long!" Local churches must expand their vision beyond the walls of the church. Authentic spirituality touches the heart of a generation that is more interested in championing the cause of those in need and advocating for justice than political interests.

GOD TALK AND POLITICS

Mingling God and party politics is a problem. It convolutes the biblical message and paints a picture that God only cares about what one political party thinks is important over another party. It undermines the biblical message that God loves everyone. It promotes special interests, preserves greed, and is likely to result in abuse of God's people.

For too long, Christians continue to blame victims for their misfortune, missing the mark on Christian love. They integrate party-based politics with faith claims. They mount pulpits and other media platforms with disparaging speeches against people who are fighting for justice. Greed often substitutes the well-being of human beings as a central focus of ministry. This was the case during slavery and Jim Crow, and it is sometimes the case today. Some prominent Christian leaders such as Franklin Graham launched attacks on the social movement of Black Lives Matter. It is appalling that the leader of one of the most significant refugee support ministries would have a kneejerk reaction that disregards human suffering. Instead of trying to understand the outcry that black lives matter equally with white lives, Graham posited a counter proposal, "All Lives Matter!" Others simply stood by idly. Perhaps they gave prayers about the crisis but did little to participate in advocating for justice on behalf of victims of injustice. Christians must not be so apt to be offended by people and cultures they do not understand. Rather, we must learn and adjust our strategies to meet the challenges of the day.

Consider the prevailing evangelical response to the NFL kneeling protests of 2017. Deeply disturbed by the police killings of unarmed African Americans and other injustices, quarterback Colin Kaepernick refused to stand for the national anthem. Instead, he led a kneeling demonstration that offended a number of evangelicals who champion a syncretistic message about "God and country." Pastor Kevin Hamm of Gardendale First Baptist Church in Alabama was one of the more prominent pastors who condemned the kneeling protest. The megachurch pastor included his slander in a Sunday morning sermon. The following is an excerpt from the sermon: "I don't mean to be insensitive . . . I just want to say you have two options. You can stay in America and help us get America back to the way God designed her. Or, if you don't like it, you can get on a boat and sail away because no one is making you stay here. Amen?"

The "God and country" message privileges the national anthem and the flag above the sacredness of human life. One wonders why any pastor wouldn't care to at least listen to the protesters' concern. Instead, Pastor Hamm and others used their platform of privilege to offer two choices. The first was to join in with President Donald Trump's promise to take the country back to some prior shining example of "God's country." Such a choice scares most African Americans and anyone who understands the horrors of injustice that paved American history, such as slavery and Jim Crow's segregation.

Pastor Hamm's second option was just as problematic as the first: "If you don't like it, you can get on a boat and sail away because no one is making you stay here." It remains unclear as to what the pastor meant by the phrase, "if you don't like it." Like what? And, of all things, he said, "get on a boat." A white preacher abominating a protest led by black people and saying "get on a boat" is most offensive, given the horror of the slave trade in which whites forced blacks to board ships to come to the New World. This sort of pervasive ideology enshrined in Christian theology is not new.

It signals a continued slave master religious mindset in contemporary American Christianity. We should not be surprised to hear that young people are questioning the relevance of the faith.

Both the crisis of faith and how we respond to the situation are crucial now more than ever. Soon, the United States of America will be a majority minority country. Right now, most young people of all races and ethnicities shrug their shoulders at racist and bigoted rhetoric. Social media and the internet have given this generation a glimpse of how big and diverse the world is. Fewer people see the world in black and white. They are becoming more interested in the many gifts of the world from a variety of people and cultures. Yet American Christianity seems stuck in the black-and-white world.

This crisis is manifested in both Christian and non-Christian circles. Christian artists such as Lecrae and Kirk Franklin have expressed frustration about the plight of black Americans who have not had their day in court. Yet at the hand of government officials, their blood stains the sidewalks.

When Lecrae went public with his frustration over police shootings of unarmed black men, the rapper was baffled by the response. Christians attacked him. He was shocked because he thought they loved him. Even Lecrae found himself second-guessing his affiliation with Christians. He was worried that there was something missing in his fidelity to a faith that seemed so distant from social pangs inflicted upon this generation.

The Dove Awards edited Kirk Franklin's award acceptance speech, cutting out his statement of solidarity with those whose heads wag in dismay in the aftermath of state supported violence against black youth and the 2016 killing of five Dallas police officers. Discouraged, Franklin decided to boycott the Dove Awards until there is a change among Christian awards and networks. He wants them to attend to the distressed communities with Christian solidarity, love, and leadership. Perhaps they are fearful that their viewers would turn off the show or perhaps they don't want to agitate their financial base. In any case, Christian television, like the award shows, distances itself from an opportunity to bear public witness to a God of justice and healing. If the current crisis of faith persists much longer without appropriate resolve, future generations in America will outright reject Christianity.

How can we expect this generation to be convinced that Christianity is about love, compassion, grace, justice, and mercy when Christian voices and institutions are either silent or uncritically supportive of systems and structures that perpetuate pain, propagate hate, proliferate exclusion, and produce death? People are hungry for a faith that

How can we expect this generation to be convinced that Christianity is about love, compassion, grace, justice, and mercy when leading Christian voices and institutions are either silent or uncritically supportive of systems and structures that perpetuate pain, propagate hate, proliferate exclusion, and produce death?

shows love and concern about injustice. People of faith must not brush off the urgent questions about the relevance of Christianity in the contemporary world. Also, we must listen to the voices that are crying out more than humdrum confessions of faith. The time has come that we return to a faith that listens to the broken world and responds with the love of Jesus. Importantly, love is not merely a hug, pat on the back, or an invitation to church. The love of Jesus is radical and confronts evil systems and structures of oppression.

SPIRITUAL WICKEDNESS AND CHRISTIAN WITNESS

In Ephesians 6, Paul speaks of spiritual warfare. The Holy Spirit empowers believers with a radical love for spiritual warfare against principalities and powers that have strongholds on human advancement. Poverty, racism, misogyny, and xenophobia are only some of the principalities that are harmful to human progress. We will know the spiritual principalities are defeated when mountains and hills are made low, the crooked straight, and the rough places plain (Isaiah 40:4; Luke 3:5). The metaphor of "leveling hills" refers to structural "isms" that will remain problematic so long as there is inequity. The powerful must relinquish power to the less powerful so that everyone has an equal playing field. "Straightening out crookedness" and "making plain rough places" speak of correcting corrupt systems.

There was a time when speaking of lived reality in spiritual terms was an unwelcomed conversation. Pentecostals were criticized for spiritualizing everything. Growing up Pentecostal, dissenters would accuse us of being so heavenly minded and of no earthly good. Perhaps we need a bit more heavenly mindedness to address the crisis of faith. Of course, by "heavenly mindedness," I am not speaking of heaven in the sweet by and by—I am speaking of the need for spiritual reflection on current social ills. Times have changed. Spirituality is much more of a welcomed conversation than it has been in the past.

SPIRITUAL BUT NOT RELIGIOUS

Millennials are drawn to spirituality in rates unparalleled to previous generations, but they are not going to church! The common confession of faith is "I am spiritual but not religious." When I taught as an adjunct professor at Sacred Heart University, students often expressed their commitment to spirituality apart from organized religion. According to a survey from Pew Research Center, only 40 percent of millennials speak favorably about religion while as many as 80 percent of them say they believe in God. The same report shows that millennials tend to be socially progressive. University of Virginia religion professor Matthew Hedstrom concludes that college students interconnect their desire for God and their pursuit of social justice. To be spiritual, for them, means to care about people in their oppressed state, advocate for the downtrodden and victims of systems that privilege some and disadvantages others, and help improve the environment. In an interview in *UVA Today*, Hedstrom says, "[Young people] want to be a part of something larger—a spiritual belief, perhaps, or a movement to improve the environment, or social justice. I don't see millennial college students today as shallow or selfish. I see a deep amount of understandable anxiety and a lot of care for the larger world and life's big questions."

This "spiritual but not religious" claim is not only on college campuses but also in society at large. What an opportunity to engage this generation!

The church was birthed by the power of the Holy Spirit and spiritual warfare is a gift from God. Biblical Christianity is more about spirituality than religion. Perhaps the cry for spirituality is more of an opportunity for the church to engage this generation than a point of departure.

FLIPPING THE SCRIPT

Given the topsy-turvy history of racial problems and the Western Christian narrative, one can understand the mushrooming suspicion about Christianity. However, a close look at slave Christianity proves instructive. Through the corridors of a difficult history, slaves teach us that there is a deep connection between spirituality and everyday life with Jesus. Faith in Jesus is about love that heals a broken world. Inherent to the faith is a nondiscriminatory fountain of eternal satisfaction, which quenches that deep-seated hunger in every soul. At a time when people are more open to spirituality than in previous generations, the Christian faith is made more attractive when it is properly understood.

Biblical faith and spirituality have historically connected people of diverse cultural backgrounds to faith in Jesus. Robert Morris, the pastor of Gateway Church, a thirty-thousand–member multiethnic church in Southlake, Texas, once preached a thought-provoking sermon titled "A Lack of Understanding." The sermon was about racism. He stated, "I believe, obviously all of us know that Jesus is the answer; but I believe the reason we still have a problem today is because of the church. I don't believe the church has taken the stand that it needs to take."

Similar to my earlier point about the church and "isms," Pastor Morris said that racism continues in the United States because the church has been apathetic to it. Holding up an Ozarka water bottle, he illustrated that people on both sides of the bottle see it from different perspectives. Those on the side of the bottle with the label can clearly read the "Ozarka" lettering. But those on the opposite side can only see the bottle—not the label. Pastor Morris explained that the racial problems that continue to permeate the faith are not a matter of malice but a result of the lack of understanding. Again, we have to listen to each other, particularly to those in pain.

As Americans regain the art of dialogue, black, white, brown, and all other Christians can work together to write a new narrative in ways that align more with the biblical faith than with colonialism. Colonial forms of Christianity have ideological links to Western colonization. They seek to enforce faith commitments through the legal system more than through the virtues of love, hospitality, and advocacy for common good. An important step in a new orientation to biblical Christianity involves confronting critical conflicts of engagement with Scripture and Christian history.

The richness of Scripture supports a culturally integrated community of faith. As we rediscover the Bible and new ways to understand the faith, we will find that the children's song is true:

Jesus loves the little children,
    all the children of the world.
Red and yellow, black and white,
    all are precious in His sight.
Jesus loves the little children of the world.

Jesus is also sensitive to their stories of injustice. He calls us to a Christlike love, compassion, and mercy. This Christian witness is much needed today!

LIVING IT OUT

Taking this book's message to the streets as well as college classrooms alerts society that God cares about ordinary people. It affirms cultural identity in a society in which the racial and ethnic identity of many has suffered attack. Black people are not mere guests of the "white man's faith," neither are they simply redeemed from the curse of blackness through Christ. Such profane ideology is a misinterpretation of Scripture.

Despite skewed historical claims, people of color have always had a powerful and prominent presence in both the Old and New Testaments. A re-imagined biblical Christianity is a gift to those who struggle with faith, identity, and life as a whole.

CHAPTER THREE

THE QUEST FOR THE SOULS

*We have men-stealers for ministers, women-whippers for missionaries,
and cradle-plunderers for church members. The man who wields the
blood-clotted cowskin during the week fills the pulpit on Sunday,
and claims to be a minister of the meek and lowly Jesus.*

FREDERICK DOUGLASS

Comedian Michael Che co-hosted the Emmys in 2018. He commented that his mother said she does not watch white award shows because they don't "thank Jesus" enough. The comedian joked that "the only white people that thank Jesus are Republicans and ex-crackheads." Many evangelicals were highly offended!

Of course, I don't know whether Che's mother really said that or not. Usually comedians use the punch line of their jokes to highlight a problem or voice a concern. Whether Che was making an assertion about the secularization of society or slandering the church (as some Christian media seemed to think) there is no denying that society has become more irreverent of religion than it used to be. One might say that the soul of society is lost in a maze of perceived social injustice, political-religious fights, and a generation's disgust of institutional religion.

In his sermon "A Knock at Midnight," Dr. Martin Luther King Jr. said, "The church must be reminded that it is not the master or the servant of the state, but rather the conscience of the state. It must be the guide and the critic of the state, and never its tool. If the church does not recapture its prophetic zeal, it will become an irrelevant social club without moral or spiritual authority." Today, we are living in a time in which the religious life of the nation is in crisis, and souls are starving for that moral and spiritual leadership that King talked about. Millennials are challenged to go it on their own while the conscience of society acquiesces its moral and spiritual authority into the hands of political expedience. All the while, alternative religious and spiritual persuasions are seizing the opportunity to fill in the gap.

MILLENNIALS AND SELF-EXPRESSION

As minorities gain power and influence on the sociopolitical front, their priority is to leverage access to self-expression. For black millennials, post-millennials, and Generation Z, this includes a demand for identity prioritization. They have also expressed their social advocacy, for example, in the #takeaknee protests and protests for gay rights, and in boycotting NFL games and the Oscars. Determined to overcome injustices of the past, black, brown, and white contemporary freedom fighters are unafraid to lift their voices on whatever platforms they have access to, such as social media, football fields, daily talk shows, concert stages, award acceptance speeches, and the streets. In this information age, they are willing to go against the grain to stand for what they believe.

Unwilling to acquiesce to a traditional faith, young people are often attracted to spiritualities that both challenge the status quo and, simultaneously, inspire them. They are eager to make a difference, reveal new ideas, and spur human progress. As a result, two things occur simultaneously:

- They discover new insights about history, culture, and traditions. This search has energized many black youth to synthesize their discoveries and become suspicious of moral philosophies that, throughout history, have systematically oppressed people.

- They tend to abandon religious traditions.

Revisioning Christianity in light of contemporary reality is necessary. The church must ask, What do we offer that young people can get excited about? A cause-driven generation has potential to ignite the church's prophetic zeal.

Competing religious sects are attuned to the spiritual hunger and gaining headway into urban communities. They are answering questions and giving young people something to be excited about.

BAITING SOULS

There is an old adage: "To be African American is to be African without memory and to be American without privilege." This quote succinctly captures a tension within the black experience. Netflix commentator Killer Mike's show called *Trigger Warning* is a platform for conversations about the state of black America. In the episode titled "New Jesus," Killer Mike interviews Pastor Creflo Dollar in an attempt to address Christianity and its relationship to black people. Early on in the episode, Killer Mike remarks confidently, "The greatest hindrance that black people have is white Jesus." He further explains to Pastor Dollar, "We [black people] have to have our Hebrew moment. We have to have our moment of 'God has chosen us, God has promised this to us, God will give this to us.'" In response, Pastor Dollar asserts, "Or we can do something more powerful than that." Excitedly, Killer Mike replies, "There can't be a better plan than that, that's the plan for us. That's the 'black people plan.'"

As young people discover more about the dark side of American history, their vision of the faith is challenged. Many share Killer Mike's suspicion that the Christian God does not care about the social pain that marginalized people experience. They have a lot of questions and are looking in all the wrong places for answers.

When people don't know who they are and where they belong, they become impressionable. Sect leaders post videos on YouTube and create websites and social media pages with tons of convincing arguments and often propaganda to attract vulnerable minds to new ideas. At different times, two millennials shared with me that they are up late at night on YouTube. In both cases, YouTube videos led them down a dark path. Both abandoned their faith. One young woman became a psychic reader of tarot cards and the other woman converted to the teachings of Science and Consciousness. The point here is that cyber technology is the new evangelism platform.

Recently, I stumbled onto a Facebook page called "Moor Info." It's a site that exclusively focuses on the black experience and covers a range of topics from politics to entertainment. I noticed a section advertising apparel. One of the items listed was a graphic T-shirt with a striking bold caption: "JESUS SLAVES." The subtle spin on "Jesus Saves" may escape the lethargic viewer, but the subtext on the shirt read, "The first slave ship used to enslave Africans was called 'Jesus.'"

It is correct that in 1564, Sir John Hawkins named his ship *Jesus of Lubeck*. He was a merchant captain who used this ship to trade slaves from 1562 to 1568. While slave trading dated back to 1515 and Hawkins's ship was used for other purposes prior to slave trading, one must not ignore the strange name of a slave ship being *Jesus of Lubeck*.

Other religions capitalize on the negative historical association of slavery with Christianity as support for their disdain of the faith. They argue that Christianity is at worst a slave supporting enterprise that commodified blacks, and at best, an outright oppressive religion. They evoke a history of professing Christians who led the slave trade business to argue that love of self cannot include loving Jesus.

Afrocentric religious movements such as Black Muslims, black nationalists, Rastafarians, and Black Hebrew Israelites stand on urban street corners and unabashedly proclaim that Christianity is the white man's religion! And, yes, young people are listening to them and joining their movements by the thousands.

This chapter offers snapshots of some of the alternative religious movements that are after the souls of urban youth. It, furthermore, argues that from the inception of the faith, Christianity has held out open arms to everyone.

ALTERNATIVE RELIGIONS AND THE SOULS OF URBAN YOUTH

Religious groups in urban centers respond directly to moral and spiritual questions. For instance, to young souls in search of connection with a higher power, they say, "You are god." Black Israelites tell young black people in search of identity, "You are the true Israelites." To the question of global black suffering, the Nation of Islam responds, "It is because the white man wants to keep you down with their religion." Along with Black Hebrew Israelites and the Nation of Islam, some other religions of urban interest are Moorish Science Temple of America and African Spiritual Systems.

Black Hebrew Israelites. The Black Hebrew Israelites offer a narrative about the "truth" of black heritage. There are indeed Africans who are genetically descendants of Jacob. Also, there are people within the African Diaspora who are Jewish converts. However, the group called Black Hebrew Israelites does not refer to either of these groups. The term *Black Hebrew Israelites* is a broad category for systems of faiths that believe African Americans are the "true" descendants of biblical Israelites. Jacob S. Dorman in his book *Chosen People: The Rise of American Black Israelite Religions* references a statement by Asiel Ben-Israel, a member of the Original Hebrew Israelites: "It isn't a religion, as such, that I follow. It's the belief that I am a descendant—and that Black people in America are descendants—of biblical Israelites. We adhere to the laws written in the Bible."

The Black Israelite message is taking foothold in many urban circles. Some are violent and others are not violent but separatists, nonetheless. From guys on the street corners to professionals to entertainers, identity infusion from the separatist group is gaining a lot of attention. For example, prominent hip-hop artist Kendrick Lamar raps in the song "Yah" that he is not black; he is an Israelite. Some people don't know what he is talking about. But others are well aware that "on the street corners of many American cities, these groups are a familiar fixture, their theatrical preaching a combustive mix of spontaneous jeremiads and confrontational engagement with passersby."

Black Israelism belief is attractive to people who are either disgruntled with the church or have a basic biblical knowledge but not a strong Christian commitment. And, like the examples in chapter one, they have a lot of questions about life, identity, and belonging. Black Israelism is complex and multifaceted as it intersects theological ideas with historical and sociological assertions.

Creating sharp distinctions and categories is also a challenge between Black Israelism and Christianity. Christianity emerges from Judaism. So, Christians have great appreciation for their Jewish heritage; Jesus was a Jew.

The African American Christian experience has always been one that has closely identified with the Israelite narrative. African slaves who embraced Christianity found solace with the enslaved children of Israel in the Exodus narrative. Negro spirituals draw on metaphors of lament, freedom, and victory from the Old Testament. Many historic denominations and churches commonly used Hebrew names such as Bethel, Shiloh, and Zion. Hence, Hebrew Israelites can be a challenge to identify and understand. However, groups that assert a literal ancestral connection between black Americans and biblical Israelites are the focus of this section.

The reasoning behind Black Hebrew Israelite identity varies depending on the group. One of their more dominant arguments, however, derives from a prooftext reading of the book of Deuteronomy, which concludes that the transatlantic slave trade and the horrors associated with it were the expression of God's judgement against black Jews for their disobedience. Chapter 28 of the book of Deuteronomy outlines blessings for obedience to the Law and curses for disobedience. Among these curses are portions that closely reflect the experience of enslaved Africans.

> The Lord will drive you and the king you set over you to a nation unknown to you or your ancestors. There you will worship other gods, gods of wood and stone. You will become a thing of horror, a byword and an object of ridicule among all the peoples where the Lord will drive you. (Deuteronomy 28:36-37)

> Because you did not serve the Lord your God joyfully and gladly in the time of prosperity, therefore in hunger and thirst, in nakedness and dire poverty, you will serve the enemies the Lord sends against you. He will put an iron yoke on your neck until he has destroyed you. The Lord will bring a nation against you from far away, from the end of the earth, like an eagle swooping down, a nation whose language you will not understand, a fierce-looking nation without respect for the old or pity for the young. (Deuteronomy 28:47-50)

Black Hebrew Israelites believe that these passages describe the forthcoming problems that black people would endure throughout the African diaspora. While the passages predict punishment for sin, they interpret them as aha moments to explain the answer to the question, Why have black people suffered so much? Additionally, the sect offers followers something to do to change the course of history—return to God and obey the Torah, and things will change!

Some Black Hebrew Israelites peacefully live out their beliefs. Others are radical and even hostile at times. An example of the more hostile expressions of the movement is the Israelite School of Universal Practical Knowledge (ISUPK) and the Israelite Church of God in Jesus Christ. The Southern Poverty Law Center (SPLC) categorizes the latter sect as a black supremacist group. And according to the ISUPK's website, this sect was founded in 1969 as a faith-based community organization to address issues facing urban America. They claim to teach "African Americans, Hispanics, and Native American Indians the true history of their people as it pertains to the Bible."

The black nationalist (or black supremacist) groups aim for high visibility and frequently position themselves on street corners and busy intersections in major urban areas such as Boston, Chicago, New York, Atlanta, Los Angeles, and Dallas to evangelize through public provocation. Their message empowers radical beliefs. For example, the SPLC reports an instance in which a black Israelite preacher slanderously predicted that white people are doomed either to a future of death or slavery. In often broken sentences or street vernacular, they win over inquisitive young minds. The SPLC quotes one of the Israelite preachers as saying, "Every white person who doesn't get killed by Christ when he returns is going into slavery." Anti-Semitic and anti-African ideologies are also common among these groups. The extremist variant of Black Hebrew Israelites can be easily identified by their combination of warlike, medieval garb and dark-colored, militant attire.

The Black Israelites are not monolithic; their belief systems exist on a continuum. As illustrated in the description of the Israelite Church of God in Jesus Christ, some are militant and aggressive connecting traditional Christian beliefs with ethnocentrism. Others believe the teachings of Christ and the basics of the gospel but hold to an exclusivist approach to Christianity. They believe that authentic Christianity is limited only to blacks. Yet, others are more inclusive and embrace Hebrew cultural practices primarily as a means of creating an identity closely aligned with biblical culture and in contrast to Western forms of Christianity. The sects attract black and Latino millennials because they offer answers to the wandering souls seeking rest and meaning in an unjust world.

African spiritual systems. Young people are on a spiritual journey to discover that which is beyond life but has everything to do with it. The search for a higher power is one level of the spiritual quest. But, the spiritual hunger also includes deeper insight into the spiritual systems that influence the created world. Indigenous African spirituality and ancestor worship offer answers to this quest.

An increasing number of millennial religious scholars, theologically trained preachers, and those who are "spiritual but not religious" pray to the ancestors and invoke the spirit world for hope and healing. The movie *Black Panther*, Beyoncé, and other pop culture trends within black culture have increased public awareness of the symbolic world of African spiritual systems. African spiritualities that see no separation between the spirit world and the natural world are relevant for the current longing to bring history and ancient spirituality for greater moral and spiritual insight.

The term *African spiritual systems* is a broad description of many religious practices from various traditional African tribes. It is important to note that there is no singular culture or spirituality in African societies. There are many; yet, ancestor worship is a dominant theme throughout the African world. They are strongly attractive, particularly, to people of African descent.

Other spiritualities like Ifa worship, Santeria (practiced among the Latin-African diaspora), and Vodun have also gained traction within these communities. These religions are attractive because they appear untainted by "whiteness." They attract followers with the promise to connect them to spiritualities that date back to indigenous African religious resources.

Moorish Science Temple of America. Founded by Noble Drew Ali in the late nineteenth century, this religious sect is often regarded as the first major presence of Islamic teaching in the African American community. The first Islamic American organization was a Moorish Science place of worship called the Holy Canaanite Temple opened in 1913 in Newark, New Jersey. Ali eventually relocated to Chicago in the 1920s and began to grow a huge following there.

At the heart of the Moorish Science message is a rejection of pejorative lingo such as "negro," "black," "African" and other terms that are believed to carry a negative connotation. My young Moorish friends shared with me their belief that black people were descendants of the Moor people who were historically powerful and ruled in Europe in the Middle Ages. They trace their ancestry through Arab history. However, Moorish Science in black America emphasizes that the Moors were people of color in Europe. In the mid-1900s, their teaching gained traction among black urbanites. In the heart of the Jim Crow Era, it conferred on them a feeling of self-worth in spite of the harsh reality that segregation created. Moorish Science revitalizing in the wake of overcriminalization in black communities, the infiltration of KKK sentiments within the nation's leadership vis-à-vis the appointment of Alt Right nationalists in the White House, and an uptick in overt racist attitudes are part of the everyday American life.

In 1928, the Moorish convention in Chicago drew about three-thousand participants and soon established temples all over the country. The Moorish Science religious text is called the Holy Koran of the Moorish Science Temple of America, which claims to contain a lost section of the Holy Koran. Moors refer to God as "Allah" and often append "Bey," "Ali," or "El" to their names. Moorish Science adherents have dwindled in number, but they are pivotal to several other religious sects that exist today. Most notably, the Nation of Islam was formed as an offshoot of Moorish Science. Wallace D. Fard Muhammad, the founder of the Nation of Islam, was initially a disciple of Noble Drew Ali before pursuing his own exploits as a religious sect leader himself.

Nation of Islam. Since the 1930s, Muhammad's Nation of Islam (NOI) has prevailed as perhaps the most influential of the black identity religious sects. Elijah Muhammed assumed leadership of the movement shortly after Muhammad founded the movement and led it until his death in 1975. The NOI grabbed the national spotlight at a pivotal time in America's history. The movement gained followers from all over the country, as it provided a narrative that helped alleviate the anxieties and frustrations experienced during an era of serious unrest.

The NOI claims that black people belonged to a lost tribe from Asia called Shabazz, and that white people were devils awaiting the coming judgment of God. Historically, this fiery message has resonated in the hearts of many, especially among young black men across America. Similar to Black Hebrew Israelite religious philosophy, the NOI offers a spiritual interpretation for the plight of black America. James Baldwin, the prolific writer and civil rights advocate, explains the relevance of the NOI during the civil rights era in his essay "Fire Next Time." Baldwin says, "One did not need to prove to a Harlem audience that all white men were devils. They were merely glad to have, at last, divine corroboration of their experience, to hear—and it was a tremendous thing to hear—that they had been lied to for all these years and generations, and that their captivity was ending, for God was black."

Similar to Moorish and Hebrew Israelite ideology, the clear and simple explanation of black suffering and white oppression as a divinely ordained phenomenon proved irresistible for many urbanites. For example, the most famous member of the NOI was Malcolm X. His first introduction to the NOI was while he was in prison. His brother Philbert wrote him an exciting letter to explain his newfound faith. Philbert described the NOI as "the natural religion for the black man." In recent years, I have spent time on the streets of Harlem. NOI continues to arrest the interest among the hungry souls that are seeking moral and spiritual direction.

It is amazing to see how fired up young converts are about their newfound faith. They don't hesitate to change their names. Men who convert to Black Hebrew Israelites are eager to dress in versions of traditional Hebrew attire. And men who convert to the NOI are eager to suit up every day, wearing the signature NOI bowtie. And, within Western societies in which telling women to dress modestly is an anathema, female Black Hebrew Israelites and members of the NOI seem to discover meaning in the "cover up" religious teachings that outweigh social norms.

WHERE TO GO FROM HERE

Humility is necessary to respond properly amid a religiously pluralized society. Very few Christians understand the complexities that are stacked in Western life. Even more find it hard to wrap their brains around the prominent role that professing Christians played in both creating and sustaining a long history of social problems. The sordid details of oppression demand the robust response from a church with what Martin Luther King Jr. calls "a prophetic zeal." Open acknowledgement of the tarnished history of Christianity must be the foundation of the prophetic zeal. The church cannot change what it does not admit. Importantly, adherents of the faith that participated in the problem have mishandled a faith that in fact possesses the internal norms to heal the very problem they created.

Christians are to be a people marked by repentance because repentance is central to the message of the good news of Jesus Christ. This repentance needs to be both personal and corporate, and as an ongoing part of Christian life. However, repentance is only a first step toward redeeming the tarnished image of the Christian faith.

We must also call to question what it means to be a biblical Christian. Confessional Christianity boasts in boldly proclaiming what they believe. But confessional Christianity is not impressive in a world in which people say one thing and live another. That is how we got where we are. Bold Christian claims have a long history of using the faith to strongarm political interests, on the one hand. If one claims that this or that idea is of God, other godly people will support it. On the other hand, bold faith announcements mask greed and selfish agendas. In other words, people have gotten away with murder (literally) when they say they are Christians. Oddly, saying that one is a Christian handed people a pass. Many have used the pass for self-aggrandizement, to build their own name, and to fortify their own wealth.

IN THE FACE OF OPPOSITION

Christians must awaken to deeper insight of biblical faith and social consciousness. Being "conscious" or "woke" has always been a nonnegotiable for blacks. W. E. B. Du Bois famously said that blacks must be "double conscious"—conscious of what it means to be black and conscious of their social location. Consciousness, or double consciousness, has produced spirited and passionate social revolutionaries. While blacks have been faithful to the American experiment, they have not always benefited from it. Their social consciousness has revealed their sacred worth against the contradictions of dominant Christianity.

Social consciousness has fortified determination, black collective identity, the embrace of cultural heritage, rejection of oppressive norms, and resistance of systemic injustice. At the heart of its varying expressions has been concern about the need for more confidence, a sense of belonging, and spirituality. Unfortunately, the vicissitudes of the black experience have sometimes shaped social consciousness in ways that appear sectarian, separatist, and tinged with extremism.

LEGACY OF THE CHURCH UNDER THREAT

Throughout history, many black Christians have defended the faith in ways that are relevant to today's skepticisms. Their public witness inspires efforts that equip women and men to reach a diverse world with a more authentic version of the gospel. For example, Frederick Douglass wrote of the pure, peaceable, and impartial Christianity of Christ. He insisted that the Christianity of Christ was different than the Christianity that forced his ancestors from Africa on ships like the *Jesus of Lubeck*. Alongside many of his peers, Douglass worked hard at building churches and Christian organizations that reflected an inclusive faith that welcomes everyone.

Following emancipation from slavery in 1863, the vigorous faith of an emancipated people led to the formation of several denominations that held high the banner of existential hope. Existential hope was necessary because the prevailing theology of hope was not very concrete. Personal piety and cultural Christian practices like going to church and being a good person would have suffocated the deeper Christian principle of tangible hope. Existential or tangible hope theology was the foundation upon which black churches became places of social healing and human development. Du Bois explains, "The negro church of today is the social center of Negro life in the United States, and the most characteristic expression of African character." Du Bois further describes the use of the church building:

> This building is the central club-house of a community of a thousand or more negroes. Various organizations meet here, the church proper, the Sunday-school, two or three insurance societies, women's societies, secret societies, and mass meetings of various kinds. Entertainments, suppers and lectures are held beside the five or six regular weekly religious services. Considerable sums of money are collected and expended there, employment is found for the idle, strangers are introduced, news is disseminated, and charity is distributed.

Du Bois paints a picture of the church as the center of gravity for developing of a flourishing community. The church has a beautiful and miraculous legacy of bearing witness to a God who cares about the wounded and oppressed. Unfortunately, this legacy has fractured over time. There is an urgent need for a renewed vision that responds to current conditions beyond the walls of the church with faithfulness to Christ, who indeed cares about people at their points of need.

LIVING IT OUT

A whole book could be written on each of the matters raised in this chapter. Rather than answering every question, I hope this chapter sheds light on the state of souls wandering in a desert of spiritual hunger in search for spiritual direction. It flashes only a small glimpse of the religious pluralism that competes with the Christian witness in the public square.

It is counterproductive for churches to exist for themselves. We Christians must strengthen our public witness to respond to prevailing cynicism and outright rejection of the faith. While we are having church, sects and cults are missionizing the communities. Christians must not be oblivious to a generation that is being attracted to alternate faiths. Churches need to be more outward-looking to respond to the intellectual and practical needs in the neighborhoods.

Long gone are the days when people attended church because it was the only option available. Now, the competition is fierce for hearts and minds. Society has nurtured young people with burning questions that provide a healthy challenge for the church. May the Holy Spirit renew and revive the faith. And may those who know the truth about Christianity lift up the name of Jesus as unifier amid far too many divisions.

May the Holy Spirit renew and revive the faith. And may those who know the truth about Christianity lift up the name of Jesus as unifier amid far too many divisions.

Souls are on a search for identity affirmation, soul care, and the spiritual quest for a power that is bigger than us. Christians must live out their faith in a way that more visibly communicates the loving Jesus who invites everyone into equal standing before the eyes of God. I hope that the current competitive faith climate shakes the church out of its complacency and awakens a nonpretentious, vibrant expression of faith.

CHAPTER FOUR

THE CHURCH AND THE SEARCH FOR IDENTITY

[Christianity] has provided theological legitimation for the overall dehumanizing denigration of black bodies.

KELLY BROWN DOUGLAS

The twenty-first century has birthed a new world with the emergence of computer technology. The world became smaller; education is finally at our fingertips thanks to online connections. Yet, with all of the advancements we enjoy today, there remains a stronghold on America's spiritual and social development. Personal piety has its place. But true revival involves both the spiritual and social at the same time.

Over the years, legislation has changed. Women and black people can vote now. Black and white people drink from the same water fountains and attend the same public schools. Yet racial attitudes, systems, and structure are often as bad as they were under the Jim Crow era. "Isms" and "phobias" such as racism, sexism, anti-Semitism, xenophobia, islamophobia, and homophobia remind us that the church still has work to do. The sense of hopelessness that accompanies a world of hate continues to fill communities.

The stats are staggering, and the reports are heart-rending. The following is a list of only a few examples. The *U.S. News & World*

Report states, "Black males are nearly three times more likely than white males to be killed when law enforcement officers use force." The Civil Rights Data Collection at the US Department of Education reports, "Black students, particularly boys, are suspended and expelled at a rate three times greater than white students." Poverty is disproportionate within communities of color, and prisons are filled with people of color, particularly black men. Additionally, research reveals the devastating news that young black children are committing suicide at record rates. It is bad enough that, among all youth, suicide is the second leading cause of death between the ages of twelve and eighteen years old. The same study shows that "the rate of suicide attempts for black youths shot up to an alarming 73 percent from 1991 to 2017. . . . Black boys also had a significant increase in the injuries they received from the attempts, which suggests that they are engaging in more lethal methods." Another study reveals that between 2001 and 2017 the rate of suicide deaths among black girls shot up an astounding 182 percent.

At one time, pain was a key motivation that led people to the church. Going to church helped to deal with life's challenges. But, with the decline of church attendance, one wonders whether church in the Western world is on the brink of extinction.

Churches are already closing. This is happening all over the Western world. Church buildings were once religious symbols of hope and spiritual spaces to call home, but now are either being torn down or converted into restaurants, night clubs, and other social venues. In a society in search of spirituality, what an unfortunate reality!

"CHURCH HURT"

Another point of concern involves the exodus of people who have been hurt in the places of healing. Space here does not permit all I would like to address about the dynamics of "church hurt." Some of the more well-known situations are priests and pastors who have sexually violated men, women, boys, and girls. This is not new. In my years of ministry, I have sat with people in their eighties who were trying to come to terms with childhood predators who they trusted as religious leaders. I have also walked with families whose children were violated by people they trusted.

Additionally, many people who grow up in the church struggle to figure out how to live their faith in light of peer pressure and personal struggles. A man shared with me how disappointed he is with the church. His bishop was indicted for numerous child sex violations over the span of forty years of ministry. The young man, who had admired the bishop, explained that when he got the news, he got depressed. That bishop had been well-known for his work in youth empowerment. He has been known for his strict religious teachings about modesty and holiness. But, more than forty testimonies allege that he was engaging in predatory sex practices all along. With deep concern about religious hypocrisy, young people are turned off when they learn that people who claim high moral standards are really hypocrites.

Another example is when award-winning gospel singer LeAndria Johnson drew attention with her public rants about the church. She felt that a legendary gospel singing pastor snubbed her in a green room. In her public statement, she said that all her life she wanted to meet him. When she finally got the chance, she was hurt when it appeared that the pastor all but ignored her. Johnson posted a video to Facebook Live lambasting the pastor and even cursing the church. Before concluding, she added that she had nothing for the church anymore. She felt it was full of phonies and hypocrites. Johnson later apologized. She also admitted that her relationship with God was strong, all the while maintaining the belief that the church has caused pain. In her experience, church people have held religious stances on issues such as doing drugs, drinking alcohol, and premarital sex, only to be guilty of hypocrisy.

The social media replies to Johnson were a mixed bag. Some were shocked by her original post of disdain for the church, especially considering her rising stardom as a gospel singer. Others chimed in with their own disparagement for the church. Whether the comments reflected shock or overt support, a common theme surfaced: people agreed that far too many Christians are hypocritical.

Could it be that contemporary churches promote religion more than they help people navigate life? In the ghettos, barrios, prisons, homeless shelters, and traps, it's sometimes hard for people to believe that they even matter to God. This is why a former bagman told me, "Doc, you've got to take the religion to the streets!"

THE NEED FOR IDENTITY FORMATION

A desire to "keep it real" drives many people into either gangs or alternative religious sects. While gangs and religious sects are not the same, they have in common a message of support. Young people are eager to be part of something that makes them feel good about themselves, invites them to a family-type community, empowers them to dream, and speaks to the problems that keep them up at night. This spiritual search stems from an innate desire to know who we are, why we are here, and our purpose. Biblical Christianity gives answers to these questions.

People need to discover who God created them to be. The silence of Christian leaders on pivotal matters gives the impression that they don't care or are not in a position to bring the healing, restoration, and triumph they preach. People desire truth. When they can't find it at home or the church, they will find alternatives to wrap their minds around the meaning of God, life, and creation. The silence of

> The silence of Christian leaders on pivotal matters gives the impression that they don't care or are not in a position to bring the healing, restoration, and triumph they preach.

public faith creates a large disconnect with many who have a hard time and desperately need Christ in their lives.

There are many people who want a better life. But they don't know how to achieve it. For example, there are many men who want to be good fathers, sons, uncles, and positive contributors to the community. But, how do they start over when they have already made a series of mistakes? Many men under fifty years old have never experienced or seen a godly man modeled before them.

There are also people who want to succeed in business, ministry, or other vocations. Others need personal and professional development. But how will they get it if they don't have personal or family connections? They need people of faith to help them. To put it in biblical typology, they need a Moses to mentor Joshua. They need an Esther to advocate for their well-being. They need an Elijah to mentor Elisha. They need a Naomi to mentor Ruth, or a Paul to mentor Timothy and Titus.

People are important. Their gifts are important, and each of their contributions to the world is equally important. When I read the devastating reports about childhood suicides, I wonder whether anyone told those children how precious they were and whether hearing that would have changed their minds. I wonder how many adult Christians tell children how important they are to God and humanity. I am convinced that we move too fast with so many distractions that we fail to let others know how important they are.

African ubuntu philosophy teaches that human beings are born out of community and sent to community. The foundational ubuntu principle is "I am because we are." This means that human identity is communal. When others remind us of our worth, they remind us that our identity is inextricably bound up in community. Apart from the community, one can neither know who he or she is, nor can one understand his or her worth.

Many people are more familiar with what the Bible says they should *not* be doing instead of finding their identity in Christ. So they don't know how important they are to Christ. Consequently, they cannot know how important they are to society. The church must care for broken people. In biblical times, the church was more than a place; it was a people who shepherded, loved, and cared for men and women.

At a coffee shop one evening, a young black woman shared that she attended a women's conference where one of the speakers preached a message that really resonated with her. The pastor spoke directly about the poverty and brokenness in her community. The pastor didn't sugarcoat it. She empowered the congregants by simply telling them how beautiful they are and that they are loved and have value. The young woman was deeply moved. The challenges she has faced had stolen her self-esteem. She said that this was the first time she had heard a message that empowered her self-worth.

When pastors pour into their congregations like that, young people might not need to run to alternative sects to gain confidence and self-determination. People who have had to battle with challenges such as rejection, low self-esteem, and socio-economic difficulties need empowerment. There is no greater empowerment than feeling that a higher power understands your pain. It is impossible to love a person if we do not go where they are.

DOES JESUS CARE ABOUT PEOPLE OF COLOR?

As a pastor, I have often been asked bizarre questions. I welcome all of them and hope that I can at least respond intelligently, even though my wisdom is weak. My knowledge is limited and often even fragmented. I received a phone call from someone who anxiously wanted to know whether the historical Jesus was white or a man of color. Given the history of racism in America, more and more young people of color are asking the same question.

Theologically speaking, it seems of little importance to know the color of the historical Jesus. Jesus loves the world and offered himself as Savior for everyone. Yet the question of historical identity is on many people's minds. Deeper than the physical features, they are concerned that perhaps Jesus can't really understand life in the ghettos and barrios. Everyone wants a Savior with whom they can relate. The musician needs to know that Jesus loves their music. The pilot needs to know that Jesus is in the airplane as it flies across the skies. The business executive needs to know that Jesus is in the boardroom to help close a deal. This is why the spirit of Christ is central to theological discourse. Jesus is present with us daily by the Holy Spirit.

But the question of divine earthly identity is not limited to whether the Holy Spirit is with us in striking deals, our occupations, or life's pain, joys, sorrows and fears. It is a tribal question. Stated plainly, did the historical Jesus look like my people or yours? A few years ago, former Fox News journalist and trained attorney Megyn Kelly poked fun at Aisha Harris's article titled "Santa Claus Should Not Be a White Man Anymore." Kelly asserted, "Get over it. Santa Claus is white. He is who he is. . . . Jesus was a white man too!" Kelly is not a ninety-year-old woman who grew up in the 1930s or 1940s. It is mindboggling that a young, educated American attorney and journalist should be so misinformed about the identity of the historical Jesus. While I am sure that Kelly needs to identify personally with Jesus like anyone else, she arrogantly dismissed any idea that Jesus was anything other than white. Saying "Jesus is white; now get over it" communicates an insensitivity to the black experience.

THE CRISIS OF IDENTITY

People want to know that they matter. So, questions from African Americans surrounding Jesus' color and facial features stem from the worry that a white Jesus would not get black people's concerns. But, as illustrated above, Kelly protects the white Jesus. It was almost as if she was saying "stop suggesting that Jesus could be black because I need him to be white." I am not a psychoanalyst. Also, it is hard to know a lot from a single comment from a journalist. But indulge me as I wonder whether Kelly has a deeper fear that if Jesus is not white, she would lose her self-confidence and, even worse, her faith.

Faith that empathizes with wounded people helps them in the healing process. I have witnessed this while ministering in some of the nation's most highly secured prisons and correctional facilities. The United States is 4.4 percent of the world population and houses nearly 23 percent of the world's prisoners. A disproportionate number of American inmates are people of color. They often want to know that Jesus can identify with them. The resurrection power of Jesus Christ presents hope for redemptive justice.

While we need prisons to help protect society from violent threats and criminals, there are far too many people who are incarcerated but need something different than a prison cell. The criminal justice system has locked away some of the world's needed potential. With proper mentoring, spiritual nurturing, education, and a better environment, more people can live into their purpose.

> **With proper mentoring, spiritual nurturing, education, and a better environment, more people can live into their purpose.**

I was a student chaplain in Atlanta when in seminary; I served as part of a prison ministry in New Haven; and then I taught in a master's degree program at Sing Sing Prison in New York. In each capacity of service, I have seen in prisoners' eyes deep regret, profound embarrassment, helplessness, and low self-esteem.

Each day that I went to class at Sing Sing Prison, there were other rooms overflowing with inmates who were intensely listening to imams from the Nation of Islam. Inmates were allowed to wear their NOI signature bowties. From what I can tell, the NOI sessions were empowering and identity forming. Crushed under the weight of poor choices or victims of circumstances, empowerment and identity formation are rich resources for prisoners.

The same is true for inmates who attend Christian gatherings. They listen for messages that will help them figure out who they are and how they should be thinking about where they are in life. They look for empowerment and spiritual formation. They need to feel close to Jesus. Imagining Jesus from their ethnic origin and or their neighborhood is comforting. Many of them don't know how to pray like church people. For instance, they need to know that Jesus is cool with them talking the way they talk, and that he understands the hard knocks of their life.

Defined by circumstances, many cannot see beyond where they are to discern who they were created to be. Many have paid their dues to society, but for one reason or another they remain incarcerated. And even when they are released from prison, most end up incarcerated again. Recidivism rates are high. American society is quick to punish but not so quick to redeem. Formerly incarcerated persons suffer from the mark of criminality on their foreheads. It's hard to move beyond mistakes that have defined them. Like everyone else, men and women with criminal records need to know their potential for greatness. They need to know who God created them to be.

I have had the privilege of preaching, teaching, and offering pastoral care to inmates. I have seen the spiritual hunger in them. Desperation for God often goes as deep as their desire to get out of prison. They often need to hear that God identifies with their trouble and there is hope on the other side of crises. They need to hear that ole-fashioned sounding but gospel truth that "trouble won't last always," and that "God will make a way out of no way." These are the messages that inspired our ancestors to believe in Jesus.

DISTRACTIONS WILL COME

Far too many people do not know who they are. There are many reasons for that. But the most important concern is that they rediscover their identity in Jesus. It is easy to be distracted from a

God-given identity when they are constantly reminded of who they are not.

For example, five months after I moved to Dallas I was hanging out with my friend Moises at a popular restaurant. An older white man came in and began flirting with some younger black women at a table next to ours. I looked up and noticed the women chuckling as if they took the man's flirts in good taste. So, I chuckled along with them.

Singling me out, the man looked at me and exclaimed, "What are you laughing at? You big ol' ape!" Oddly, I was both startled and unsurprised at the same time. I swallowed hard. My eyes crossed, but this time I kept my cool.

> Human advancement cannot occur by simply changing laws, job opportunities, and examples of black achievements. The church has a role to play in helping to shift the attitudes and systems that sustain the plague of hopelessness and despair.

Moises said, "Bro, are you going to let him call you that?!" He immediately told the server what happened. Shocked and highly offended, she immediately reported it to the manager. The manager, who was hanging out near the bar at the time, ran over, and immediately dismissed the man and his family.

I was startled when the man called me an ape. But I could only imagine how crushed a person who is poor, less formally educated, or has a criminal record would be to be called names or treated poorly. It would only remind them of who they are not, leaving them wondering if they have any value. Clearly, we still live in a world in which prideful people feel it is okay to demean others and call them horrible names. From prisons to corporate America, self-discovery is a challenge. And some people do not respond well when others treat them in a way that makes them feel less than a human being.

A DEEPER STRUCTURAL PROBLEM

Name calling is symptomatic of deeper structural sins that are too often ignored among Bible-toting Christians. The church must lead in the support of human dignity. This means that we must publicly rebuke politicians who demean God's people with perverted references and name calling. For example, evangelical Christians missed an opportunity to attend to the identity crisis when President Donald Trump called the black-led NFL kneeling protestors "sons of b——s." Instead, many of them sided with the president. They criticized the protestors, once again missing an opportunity to listen to the wounded voices. The church has a role to play in helping to shift the attitudes and systems that sustain the plague of hopelessness and despair.

The deeper structural problem is that the more money a person has, the greater their moral defense. Christians who uncritically support leaders because they have their proverbial "hands in their pockets" betray the faith. Having money does not bring the healing our world needs. Many people have money, but it can't buy them peace. It can't buy joy. And it does not heal the social distresses that people feel.

American functionalism is a social system in which people who move up the social ladder must play by the rules. If women and people of color are to move up, they must play by the rules. They don't get to change the rules and keep moving up! Laura Ingraham crystalized this assumption on Fox News in response to LeBron James's political commentary when she mounted on white privilege and chastised James for "talking politics" during an interview. James expressed that he feels that the president of the United States does not care for the people. Defending one of the most unbridled presidents in American history, Ingraham felt that the basketball player should have stuck to the script and refrained from any criticism of the president. She exclaimed, "Keep the political comments to yourselves. . . . Shut up and dribble." Ingraham is a journalist, but she assumed the authority to put James in his "place." This struck a racial chord among many voters. It illustrated a deeper concern that there are people who feel they have the right to reprimand a man of color for sharing his opinion about American leadership.

Racial aggression isn't experienced exclusively in the limelight. Someone graffitied a racial slur on James's Los Angeles home. James responded to Ingraham's rebuke saying, "The best thing she did was help me create more awareness.... We will definitely not shut up and dribble.... I mean too much to society, too much to the youth, too much to so many kids who feel like they don't have a way out."

Colin Kaepernick has struggled to re-enter the NFL after upsetting social structures with his kneeling protest. Historically, people of color are supposed to keep their heads low and do as they are told or else they may pay a steep price. The contemporary social crisis raises questions about human worth and purpose. James has money and unparalleled talent on the basketball court, but Ingraham reminded him that his opinion about how society is run is not of as much value as his ability to play ball. Kaepernick has money and unparalleled talent on the football field, but regardless of his noble cause, he led a protest that was percieved as an insult to American patriotism. And even some Bible-toting evangelicals dismissed a good cause.

Contrary to forces that seek to hold one back, the story of the incarnation teaches us that God came among us to propel us forward. Jesus came among a particular people at a particular time and had their experience. All of creation matters and God hears to the voices that cry for help.

HOW CAN THE CHURCH ADDRESS THE IDENTITY CRISIS?

With fewer men present in many American families, the question of identity rises to prominence. Children should learn who they are at home. But it is hard to fully embrace identity when families are broken. Young people suffer from unresolved identity problems. At any age, one might experience an identity crisis. Trauma and life-changing situations often trigger identity crises. However, the type of identity crisis of concern is Erik Erikson's stage of development wherein teenagers usually resolve their identity crisis by adulthood. Perhaps people are not resolving their adolescent identity crises within the common rhythm they used to or they are having more frequent identity crisis cycles. In either case, adults are struggling with unresolved identity crises. It is hard to manage life without a firm grip on who you are. Young adults who battle with an unresolved identity crisis are vulnerable for failure. It

> **Christ invites a world in search of identity to discover who they are in him.**

may not be surprising, moreover, that a survey by the US Department of Justice showed that 39 percent of jail inmates lived in mother-only (father-absent) households.

When properly understood, Christianity offers redemption for brokenness. The Christian faith invites everyone to divine identity. Peter reminds believers that "he who called you is holy, so be holy in all you do; for it is written: 'Be holy, because I am holy'" (1 Peter 1:15-16). In other words, Christ is God's invitation to every human being, regardless of their family situation, social location, ethnic identity, or past life. The invitation is to be like God. What an amazing opportunity! Paul explains that anyone who is in Christ is a new creation (2 Corinthians 5:17). The invitation does not extend only to those with high church attendance and regular Bible reading plans, but to everyone, including the people on street corners, in prison, or the people who are struggling with addictions and mental illness. Christ invites a world in search of identity to discover who they are in him. A divine belonging is the unique gift the church must offer to the world.

Jesus could have come into this world in a much grander way. Trumpets could have sounded as he slowly descended from heaven. But Jesus came as a reflection of the people that he came to save. He emptied himself of divine privilege and left a heavenly home to live with us (Philippians 2:5-11). Jesus always had a heart for the underprivileged, often speaking up for the poor, healing the sick (Mark 3:1-6), and demonstrating how his followers should treat and respect other people.

Jesus is all about love and unity. His followers must live out his main message to be called Jesus' disciples. Jesus said, "A new command I give you: Love one another. As I have loved you, so you must love one another" (John 13:34). This means that Christians must not be known more for what they believe or their political affiliations than their love. The early church was built on love. It is crucial that Christians demonstrate what it looks like to manifest the fruit of love, including kindness, patience, self-control, goodness, faithfulness, joy, peace, and endurance (Galatians 5:22-23). When Christians show the fruit of unconditional love, we draw others to the discovery of who they are in Christ.

LIVING IT OUT

Lives are at stake and the future of the world depends on how Christians unify to fight against injustice. When non-Christians can clearly see the problem with the "isms" and "phobias," the faith appears more blinding than revealing. People need to know who they are in Christ. Jesus calls his followers to open the eyes of the blind. There are many blinded not only to who they are but also to what Christ has to offer. Sharing the love of Christ with others is more than an invitation to church or an invitation to baptism or to say the sinner's prayer. It involves being present with people in rejection so they may experience the expression of divine hope in their time of need.

Come Holy Spirit. Heal the church and society. Help us see more clearly so the world will discover its potential as we submit to your Word.

PART TWO

HAVE WE BEEN
TAUGHT TO MISREAD
THE BIBLE?

CHAPTER FIVE

THE CHRISTIAN'S
SCANDALOUS THINKING

Christianity has given rise to race-based thinking in the Western World.

Sameer Yadav

Much of Christian thinking has been shaped by poor biblical interpretation rather than historical, contextual readings of Scripture. Some of my most intense arguments with Christians have been around matters of interpretation and not the actual biblical text in question. When I was in college, a young waiter I knew from a local restaurant who loved to discuss the Bible wanted to talk about the baptism of the Spirit. She explained something she had been reading. I struggled to follow her interpretation of the passage. When she whipped out a study Bible to prove her point, I noticed that she was relying on the commentary footnotes. This new Bible student was being shaped by certain interpretations of Scripture more than Scripture itself. That was my first clue that commentators have guided much of today's scandalous thinking about the Bible.

While study aids are helpful, contemporary scholars note that for centuries many prominent theologians and biblical commentators subtly insert their opinions that force unfounded meaning upon the text. Sometimes it does not seem to make a big difference. But other times, subtle insertions have significant consequences for Christian thinking. Since the 1960s, a long line of scholars including but not limited to James H. Cone, Cain Hope Felder, Brian K. Blount, Leonard Lovett, Renita J. Weems, Elisabeth Schüssler Fiorenza, and others have stood on the margins of theological scholarship and criticized how commentaries and theological education have, for centuries, shaped racially biased and gender oppressive biblical interpretation. For a long time, their criticisms were brushed off as radical and unfounded because they did not align with mainstream Christian thought.

To have a serious conversation about biblical interpretation, one must confront the problem of colonial readings of Scripture that have permeated Western Christian history since the sixteenth century. A common topic of interpretive difficulty concerns the phrase, "Slaves, obey your earthly masters" (Ephesians 6:5; Colossians 3:22). During slavery, slave masters used these passages as religious yokes to justify their abuse of black slaves. It is crucial to understand how hegemonic ideas have abused biblical interpretation. It is even more important to re-read Scripture for its historical-contextual meaning and its appropriateness in Christian sensitivity to ethnic and cultural diversity. The Bible is more culturally inclusive than many people think. In a society with increased division, the message of God in Christ is one that equalizes all people. The message is that everyone is an equal reflection of God's image in the world. No one person or group of people is better than another!

THE BIBLE AND EVERYDAY QUESTIONS

For too long, residual effects of colonial readings have plagued the Christian mind. Subconsciously, Christians privilege some people and devalue others. Society has not overcome the divisions that separate whites and blacks. While there are some racially integrated churches, one of the most segregated units in society is the church. Think about it. People who share the same language, schools, restaurants, cities, religion, and Bible still have different assumptions about what worship and religious life should look like! In large part, we accept this reality because old theological assumptions continue to separate God's people in unprecedented ways. If worship space were the only issue, the problem might not be so large. The ramifications of segregated worship have to do with sustaining the ideological frameworks that fostered segregation in the first place—so-called Christian thinking that privileged some and oppressed others.

The late Katie Geneva Cannon was the first black woman to be ordained in the Presbyterian Church (USA) and the first black woman to earn a PhD from Union Theological Seminary in New York. As a child in the church, she often wondered why this "good God" she learned about in her Sunday school class let black people suffer. When she was twelve years old, she worked for a white family and questioned again why the responsibility fell on her to work for them and take care of their children. The job paradigm was never the other way around. Blacks working for whites shaped black Christian thinking. But Cannon knew something was not right about this societal structure because it violated the core of her personal experience with God. The God she knew did not make blacks subservient to other human beings. While many blacks held this deep conviction, they struggled to grasp the political power to change their situation.

Cannon enrolled in seminary in search of her own voice. But she found herself under the uncomfortable encumbrance of training that did not value her views very much. She submitted a theology paper to Professor Beverly Harrison and admitted that she found it burdensome submitting to the ideological control of authors such as Kierkegaard, Niebuhr, and Tillich. The professor handed back the paper and challenged Cannon to use her experience and insights to frame a voice the world had not yet heard. Professor Harrison helped Cannon see that a black woman from the South could utilize her culture and context as authentic mechanisms through which God, the Bible, and justice coexist to affirm both her humanity and sanctity as a black woman of God. A light went on in Cannon's head! Society had already forged a meaning of God, the Bible, and self that were neither truly of God nor a true reflection of Cannon's identity.

Experience matters in shaping the Christian mind. Colonial approaches reject the notion that new interpretations of Scripture emerge when both the biblical context and contemporary context of vast cultural diversities meet. Biblical scholar Brian Blount explains:

> **Experience matters in shaping the Christian mind.**

> Instead of immediately rejecting another culture's reading of (a text) as a corrupted, self-interested, and therefore biased eisegesis, the cultural reader recognizes that the only way to expand meaning is to value the fact that readers in different cultures will access meaning potential in ways that, while different, may well be no less worthy, no less meaningful.

However, until today, white and male hegemony in Christian thought continues to strongarm discussions about what is biblically and theologically correct.

Particularly, evangelical Christian thinking is shaped by an assumption that truth is objective, and by the arrogance of knowing what that truth is and how to live it out. Everything else is thought to be a "deviation." I believe truth is an objective truth. God is objective in that God is impartial, never changing, and the highest being by which all things were created. However, human beings live in observance of God from their positions of experience. An illustration from my professor Harold Attridge at Yale Divinity School has stuck with me: Our relation to truth may be described by a multiangled prism with truth in the center. Depending on the angle one looks at it, the color differs. The substance of the center remains, but the angle of view changes perception.

Moreover, the traditional Christian claim on knowing objective truth and how to live it out privileges certain ways of thinking over others. This is the epistemological assassin that has often demonized black peoples' way of relating to the world that destabilized their sense of belonging during slavery and Jim Crow. When one is made to think that they are a problem and their way of relating to the world is problematic, it places them at the mercy of their fixer. This interpretive framework has spread around the globe as missionaries and colonizers have worked vigorously to advance their own cultural identity in the name of reaching non-Christians. For them, Christianity became the pedagogical strategy to housebreak black slaves. The colonizers discovered that the indigenously religious could be controlled by religion, which made it easier to hold them in bondage.

EUROCENTRISM IN MINISTRY TRAINING

Biblical scholar Cain Hope Felder asserts, "What passes for normative hermeneutics is in fact, white, male, Eurocentric hermeneutics." This is not to suggest that white scholars are unable to interpret the Bible or practice the art of theology. Of course, they can and they must. Neither is my point to lift black interpretation as superior to others. That would actually undermine my argument for diverse interpretive methods. However, the history of biblical interpretation is laced with religious oppression rooted in the harmful mishandling of the Bible.

It is a scandalous reality that systems excluding marginal voices have replaced God's active voice in the church. Interpretive norms sanctified oppression and made segregation a part of American Christian practice. In what world would someone think that a singular system of study should assume ultimate authority over all others and that diverse methods are somehow invalid or even toxic? Yet, this approach has plagued Christian thinking all over the world for centuries. Twenty-first century young people are tired of prodding their brains to make sense of it. They are closing the Bible because of insane interpretations that have beleaguered the Christian mind. They are walking away from the church wondering if it is even relevant in today's world. As that old saying goes, "They are throwing out the baby with the bath water." Biblical scholar and pastor William Myers explains,

> [Those who train ministers] presuppose a Eurocentric worldview and approach to biblical interpretation. The (academic) books emphasize selected events in the history of interpretation (the Reformation, the Enlightenment); selected methodological concerns (biblical criticism in general and historical-critical method in particular); or selected hermeneutical motifs (authorial intent, inspiration, inerrancy, propositional revelation).

For people to understand and appreciate the Bible, they must understand their own history—not adopt a methodology centered around other points of view. An oppressive past follows us, albeit its form has been modified so as not to appear overt. Consider how oppression comes in so many forms. For example, the way theology and biblical studies are taught in the church and the academy advantage eighteenth- and nineteenth-century Western ways of thinking over other diverse ways of thinking. By doing so, the schools sustain colonial superstructures that marginalize the hard work African American and other ethnic or racial minority scholars have done to advance new insights into a God who privileges underprivileged people by placing them on an equal playing field with all others. As a result of colonization in the shaping of the Christian mind, legalized, passive oppression continues by silencing voices in the church.

THE "YESSAH" RELIGIOUS MENTALITY

The Christian scandal is exacerbated when historically marginalized people uncritically rationalize their own oppression as "the Christian way." Or, even worse, when they stand idly by and accept oppression, saying "Well, the Lord is in control." That kind of biblical interpretation dates back to slavery. Ex-slave preacher Frederick Douglass said,

> Between the Christianity of this land, and the Christianity of Christ, I recognize the widest possible difference—so wide, that to receive the one as good, pure, and holy, is of necessity to reject the other as bad, corrupt and wicked. To be the friend of the one, is of necessity to be the enemy of the other. I love the pure, peaceable, and impartial Christian of Christ: therefore hate the corrupt, slaveholding, women-whipping, cradle-plundering, partial and hypocritical Christianity of the land. . . . I look upon it as the climax of all misnomers, the boldest of all frauds, and the grossest of all libels. Never was there a clearer case of "stealing the livery of the court of heaven to serve the devil in." I am filled with unutterable loathing when I contemplate the religious pomp and show, together with the horrible inconsistencies, which everywhere surround me.

Douglass somehow separated his own commitment to Christ from the slave master's religion. His own experience with God was so profound that he read the Bible for himself and applied a religious and social critique on the state of so-called Christianity during slavery. Douglass was convinced that the Christian faith of the Bible offers solutions, hope, love, compassion, and affirmation for all people. So, he decided to use his gifts to participate in God's work of defeating the evil of slavery.

In today's society, scandalous thinking cripples people from living out their purpose. We learn from Douglass and others that acquiescing to what life throws our way is scandalous thinking. God is, rather, calling for us to be incarnational.

The incarnation is about a God who came among us in Jesus Christ and set up residence in our neighborhoods (John 1:14). This means that the Christian mind properly formed is inherently about a God who shows up in our world to realize God's hope, love, compassion, and impartiality for all people.

BEYOND SPIRITUAL COLONIZATION

While blatant forms of colonization ended many years ago, ideological and spiritual colonization persists. In the West, colonization of ideas occurs when people of color are made to think that their ideas are less noble than those of white people. Spiritual colonization bears its resemblance; only worse because it is mental and spiritual. The presence of God among God's people—not powerful human beings—brings spiritual legitimacy.

> The presence of God among God's people—not powerful human beings—brings spiritual legitimacy.

Here's a simple example of cultural bias in the development of two of the leading study Bibles on the market—the English Standard Version Study Bible and the HarperCollins Study Bible of the New Revised Standard Version. Both translations claim to be authoritative and the study notes included are penned by some of the world's leading scholars. Without exception, the oversight editorial team for both volumes are white men that are trained in the male-dominant, Eurocentric model of biblical interpretation. They are fine scholars, but their perspectives are limited to their own context and ideology. There remains a dire need for commentaries from people of color and from female perspectives.

LET'S THINK ABOUT THIS

Traditional theological education has limited biblical interpretation to studying original languages, decolorization of biblical characters, and assigning presuppositions, agendas, and male-dominant biases.

The process can become very complex. For those of us who have studied biblical languages, it is a very humbling process. Even still, there is another element blindly overlooked—the modern worldview of the interpreter diving into the ancient culture and texts.

Proper theological thinking is a melding of both the primitive world that we are investigating and the modern views of the ones peering deeply into the ancient past. The two inform how we should think about God and the world. If the ancient text is only communicating with a Eurocentric worldview, the interpretation that follows will be a Eurocentric message to its hearers, which ends up being unhealthy for the majority of the world's population.

We understand ancient cultures and modern texts based on our questions, prejudices, assumptions, biases, and a host of other factors that make us interpreters. For example, my brother Alonzo is a trained musician. He reads a piece of music with musical knowledge and skills. This naturally influences the way he interprets a piece. Those who are not musically trained interpret arrangements as well. They may read the same piece of music as my brother, attempt to understand what the arranger was trying to do with the piece, and even grasp what was going on in the composer's life at the time that the piece was composed. But even with all of that hard work, the trained and untrained listeners' interpretive lenses influence the way they understand a piece of music.

The way that we handle the Bible is similar. We must not continue to trick ourselves into thinking that people's experiences are not important when interpreting Scripture. Of course, we must be faithful to the text, but human experience is as a significant part of interpreting the Word of God in Scripture. Yet, almost without fail, Western European models of biblical interpretation assume the dominant voice heard in American liberal and conservative, Catholic and Evangelical churches.

For example, in the Old Testament story of Abraham and Sarah, God promises Abraham that he and Sarah will have a baby even though they are very old. In a plot twist—though, one well within the normal activity of this primitive culture—Sarah suggests that Abraham have a baby with one of their slaves named Hagar. It's a set of circumstances that seems bizarre to modern readers, but it was not an uncommon practice at the time for a man to continue his family lineage in that way.

As things turn out, Abraham impregnates Hagar. Contemporary readers might call it an example of sex slavery! At any rate, Hagar births a male child named Ishmael. God never condemns the cultural practice of slavery in the story or the use of the female slave as a sex object. It was as normal to the context as it was for Thomas Jefferson to own Sally Hemings and sexualize her. In both the NRSV and ESV Study Bibles mentioned earlier, the editors' commentary notes are silent on the practice of slave ownership and the blatant sexual abuse in the narrative. Why is this the case? Could it be that the white male commentators are oblivious to what it feels like to live in oppression and under the abuse of power? How might the commentary's notes on this or that particular passage have differed if a slave, refugee, undocumented immigrant, black or brown person, or a woman wrote the commentary?

As the story progresses, God rebukes Abraham and Sarah for their attempts to circumvent God's plan by choosing the culturally acceptable way of having a child over the faith-centered one. Based on God's rebuke, the couple realized that Ishmael is not the child they were promised as an heir. Instead, as senior citizens, God promises once again to give them a son together. The story tells us that a miracle takes place and Abraham and Sarah have their first child together—Isaac. Often, Abraham is lifted as the hero in the text. But there is far greater depth to the story than that.

Because of the experiences of our ancestors and parents, for example, black people, refugees, undocumented immigrants, or abused women may read this text with particular interest in the plight of the slave girl and the child. The Bible tells us that Sarah grows jealous of Hagar and Ishmael. She insists that they be evicted from Abraham's wealthy property with no equivalent of a trust, will, insurance, or 529 plan. Abraham, the father of Ishmael, appears to be a weak and voiceless bystander as the child and his mother are sent into the desert to face what most would have assumed to be their inevitable death. Although the story looks bleak, God intervenes in the hopeless situation and miraculously provides nourishment for Hagar and the child. God blessed the boy with a promising future. If it were not for God breaking into this human story of marginalization, abandonment, and fatherlessness, perhaps blacks, refugees, undocumented persons, or abused women would find it hard to digest the story.

For scholars interested in the formation of the Jewish people, this story has a rich and deep meaning. Without the miraculous provision of a child between two aged people, Isaac would have never been born. From this child, the Hebrew people—the nation of Israel—are said to have eventually emerged. The story of an impossible childbirth is regularly celebrated in the church as an example of God's capacity to keep covenant promises, even if it means intervening in the form of miracles. Nothing is impossible for God!

But the story has other characters besides Abraham, Sarah, and Isaac. Also, the reader's worldview determines how they are understood as well as what level of emphasis is placed on each of them. For the Hebrew people, Hagar and Ishmael are classified as products of a faithless system. They are seen as "less than" because Abraham and Sarah determined they were not connected to the promise of God for their own future, which made them disposable. Hagar, a slave owned for the pleasure of others, could be removed from the community simply because of her negligible status within Abraham and Sarah's circle of influence. It did not matter that she was the mother of Abraham's child—she was expendable.

CONTEXTUAL QUESTIONS AND BIBLICAL INTERPRETATION

Fast forward a few thousand years to the apostle Paul and his letter to the believers in Galatia. He interprets the Genesis narrative about Abraham, Sarah, Hagar, and the birth of their sons through the eyes of a first-century Jew with an audience of Roman citizens (Galatians 4:21-31). Importantly, Paul is a descendent of Sarah's son Isaac and presents the story as a Christian metaphor. He asserts that those who try to live for God by legislation rather than by faith are comparable to Abraham taking upon himself to have Ishmael by his maid.

Paul explains Sarah's son Isaac's birth as living by faith and Hagar's son Ishmael as a product of trying to fulfill God's promises on his own terms. He implies that our choices to follow flesh-driven choices will produce sinful outcomes. So, we should ignore impulses of the flesh to live according to God's promises. This is Paul's theological interpretation of the story to illustrate the seriousness of faith over trying to work things out on our own.

Here the author (Paul) reads the ancient Hebrew narrative through his contextual lens and with close attention to the theological metaphor embedded for first century Christian insight. Again, black people, refugees, undocumented immigrants, or abused women enjoy the benefit of Paul's main point about living by faith. But they also would likely focus on the horror surrounding the treatment and fate of the slave.

The reader's context shapes the way in which one tells and understands the story. Paul's focused audience would connect with his reading of the story. Their main question is about what it takes to be a part of the Christian family. Should they be circumcised or not? But another audience at another time in history may have questions about the abuse of power.

THE TYRANNY OF CONTEXTUAL INTERPRETATION

Concerns about power and oppression glare in our contemporary world. Christian interpreters would miss an opportunity for ministry if they overlooked it. Where is the justice for Hagar? A person sensitive to suffering does not quickly rejoice because God miraculously provided for her and her son. They are much more empathetic and take the time to attend to the pain that Hagar must have felt as she is taken against her will, used as a sex slave, and forced to bear a child because a man wanted an heir in his old age. Then, when the couple miraculously birthed a son on their own, they evicted the slave and her child. Hagar became a single mother to care for her child alone. She had no option but to prepare for what appeared to be an inevitable death. But God cared for the woman and the child! Reading the story this way highlights a God who cares for people who are used and abused and for battered women and single mothers.

Indeed, life experiences inform the questions we bring to the biblical text. Scripture invites all of God's children to the theological task of connecting the narrative of the biblical text with the reader's lived experience. So, when the black, brown, or the female interpreter reads the text, the narrative is not a Jewish or Arab story, but one of millions of people of color or women who know what it's like to experience life like Hagar.

We must be careful not to make contextual interpretations normative. It limits the Spirit's work of translating the internal norms of God's love into the many contexts of God's diverse universe. An example of this is the idea that America is "the land of the free and home of the brave." It was rooted in an interpretation of the life of Abraham—a man who left his homeland in search of a land that God promised him. The settlers believed that the New World could be a place where God's kingdom could be established. Implicit in the assumption was that their small tribe of people were all God had to work with. So, as God did with Abraham's descendants, a new nation could be formed.

Note that in their biblical interpretation, natives already in the land that Europeans overtook to create America were not free to call it home. And, until today, there are systems in place to limit who is welcome to experience American freedom. So, the ideal America was never for all of God's children. The question is not about who we say we are. The question is about what we mean by what we say. And, the American ideal has always been implicitly exclusionary. Placing biblical interpretation primarily in the hands of privileged people presents God's word in theologically myopic and often tyrannical ways.

> Placing biblical interpretation primarily in the hands of privileged people presents God's word in theologically myopic and often tyrannical ways.

America is not the first to practice theological conquest. European ideals have a longstanding history of empowering nations to expand to other parts of the globe, colonizing ethnic groups, and marginalizing their status as human beings. Their religious crutch in the pursuit of power were often "certain reading[s] of the Abrahamic myth in Genesis, a reading that inspired European settlers to think that, as with Abraham, God was intimately involved with them, ordaining their affairs and ordering their movement into their 'new world.'"

CONTEXTUAL AND ARBITRARY INTERPRETATION ARE NOT THE SAME

Biblical scholar Brian K. Blount explains that a biblical text "should not be interpreted arbitrarily according to the needs of whatever populace is studying it at any particular moment." Contextual reading is not making the Bible say whatever one wants it to say. There are historical and literary criteria that restrict certain meanings of texts and should provide boundaries around what a passage actually says. The generally promoted standard of measurement, however, has been a Eurocentric standard that Blount calls "restrictive" rather than "inclusive." He explains that the problem has been that when one uses an approach to biblical interpretation that does not match the traditional standards of European scholars, the interpreter and audience are supposed to be "altered appropriately" to meet the status quo.

An example is how interpretations of Romans 13:1-3 have been systematized in American religious life. Paul writes about the authority of government and the expectation that followers of Christ will honor and observe the powers that have been established by God's order. The instruction sounds obvious and practical to the naked eye, but:

- What happens if government, or another system of power, operates from an abusive or oppressive posture?
- What if the political system attempts to enact policies that marginalize the personhood of an individual or are contrary to the teachings of Jesus Christ?

For hundreds of years, the passage has been used to justify governmental power plays to oppress the weak. It is still being used in this way. In the national debate about what to do about the immigration crisis at the American southern border, Attorney General Jeff Sessions referenced Romans 13 as religious rationale for separating immigrant parents from their children. The unyielding application of law and order undermined any proposal for compassion and hospitality. The Attorney General argued that the undocumented mostly brown people from the Spanish-speaking world get what they

> When multiple voices are part of biblical interpretation, the Bible comes alive for many different people from many different life situations, and with many different skillsets and levels of education.

deserve. And anyone who disagrees with the family separation policies needs to take it up with Romans 13.

It is funny how the powerful often interpret Scripture to hold others down rather than to disempower themselves; to say they are right, and others are wrong. This problematic approach to interpretation first of all exemplifies why we need the Holy Spirit. Secondly, we need a variety of interpreters to participate in the journey to understand the richness of God's Word. When multiple voices are part of interpretation, the Bible comes alive for many different people from many different life situations with many different skillsets and levels of education.

LIVING IT OUT

People from every nation, culture, and creed, and people from all types of backgrounds and with many life stories bring concerns and questions to Bible study. The church must take all of their concerns into account. Their questions are gifts that make Bible study interesting and relevant to lived experience. Bearing public witness (Acts 1:8) requires listening to the cries of God's diverse people and attending to the solutions that God's Word brings to every creature.

For those looking to broaden their study and deepen their insight into how God's Word speaks to such a gigantic world with many people and experiences, God may be calling you to formal theological training.

1. We need more people of color to learn original biblical languages (Hebrew, Aramaic, and Greek) and pursue biblical scholarship.

2. We need theological research in conjunction with ongoing dialogue between scholars and pastors.

3. We need to learn new biblical interpretation methods.

4. We need to stop relying so much on commentaries, using them as tools but not as the final authority in biblical interpretation.

5. We need more people of color, people with many life experiences, and women to participate in theological education.

CHAPTER SIX

THE COLOR OF THE BIBLE

*The worlds of both the Old and New Testaments were ethnically diverse
and richly textured by an assortment of cultures, languages, and customs.*

E. RANDOLPH RICHARDS AND BRANDON J. O'BRIEN

T hose who believe the myth that Christianity is the white man's
religion also believe that the Bible is the white man's book. At
the heart of this claim lies two assumptions. One is that Christianity has been historically used in South Africa, South America,
Central America, the Caribbean, and the United States of America
to prop up systems of oppression. The other assumption is that
Jesus, Moses, and the rest of the cast of the Bible were white. Of
course, these are not new claims or assumptions. The Bible has
been under suspicion in every place people have suffered under the
pressure of select Bible verses. In this chapter, I will address the
color of the Bible, specifically considering the ruling assumption
that most biblical characters had fair skin, straight hair, etc.

There's an old story given to us by the twentieth-century writer
Franz Kafka that goes something like this: leopards routinely break
into the temple and drink up all the wine in the sacrificial cups. The
leopards do this over and over again, until finally it becomes part
of the ritual. Though simple, Kafka's story offers a parable for how
rituals are developed through repetition to the extent that no one

questions the correctness or even the implications at play. The marriage between Christianity and whiteness is a lot like Kafka's story. For thousands of years Western Europeans co-mingled their ideas with Christian rhetoric. Then in the nineteenth century they widely distributed a picture of a white Jesus. Without realizing it, people in diverse cultures started buying into a faith and images of the faith that deified whiteness. Subliminally, the characters in the Bible became white, and the prominent images of baby Jesus, Jesus the teacher, and the crucified Christ that were all white were accepted without question.

Let's pause and break down some important definitions. When talking about the color of the Bible, it's easy to fall back on terms such as *race*, *ethnicity*, or even *nationality*. But these terms are tricky to apply to an ancient Near Eastern context. Our modern categories around race did not exist two thousand years ago. The meaning of these terms depends on the social situation from which they emerge, which was long after Jesus' death. We must be careful not to read our contemporary categories into ancient settings. As Craig Prentiss notes in his book on the formation of race in Christianity, "Biblical characters lived in an ancient Semitic, Mediterranean, and North African world, one in which modern understandings of 'white' and 'black' would have been meaningless."

On the one hand, we must be careful not to read our modern categories of race back into the Bible too quickly. But on the other hand, the Bible was itself used by slave owners in America to *create* categories of race, whiteness, and blackness. The use of the Bible to create concepts of blackness and whiteness becomes even more perplexing when one considers that, in fact, very few people in the Bible had white skin. In fact, most of the central figures in the Bible were people of color and were born in difficult circumstances, including many of the biblical patriarchs and prophets stretching from Abraham to David and, yes, Jesus.

PEOPLE OF COLOR IN THE BIBLE

Imagine a little dark-skinned baby born to an unmarried peasant girl named Mary. Impregnated under odd circumstances, Mary had already resisted any potential temptation to terminate her pregnancy. Then, shortly after the baby's birth, his poor, dark-skinned mom and stepdad were warned to flee as refugees to Egypt because of Herod's threat of infanticide.

Undoubtedly, they were embarrassed, frustrated, and stressed out; but, deep down they knew their baby's purpose was far bigger than his birth conditions. He was worth fighting for!

Now, snap back.

That image is closer to historical accuracy. With a backdrop of a version of Christianity that has supported hostility against dark-skinned people, teen mothers, and refugees, and often lacks support for the unborn and newborn babies, it is hard to believe that Jesus was a dark-skinned, protected child of an unmarried teenager and a refugee.

Additionally, most of the authors of the books of the Bible were people of color. In the New Testament, the author of the Gospel of Mark was a Jew from Cyrene, which was located in the modern northeast region of Libya. Most scholars believe that the book of Mark was the first of the Gospel writings, and that the Gospels of Matthew and Luke use Mark as a guide for their outline. This would mean that the author of the first Synoptic Gospel was an African Jew. Also, although the book of Hebrews does not have an author's signature, many scholars believe that Apollos wrote Hebrews. If this is the case, then Hebrews was also written by an African because Apollos was an Egyptian Jew from Alexandria.

ETHNIC MIXING IN THE BIBLE

The Bible features members from a kaleidoscope of ethnicities. From Israelites to Kushites, Egyptians to Babylonians, Romans to Jews, and North Africans to Greeks, the Bible contains rich ethnic threads with accompanying ideological influences. Most importantly, the Bible not only features an ethnically diverse cast of characters, but also a good chunk of the Hebrew Bible is dedicated to *encouraging* diversity, ethnic mixing, and border crossing. The Bible tells us repeatedly that the Lord favors those who leave the limits of their ethnic boundaries. In fact, God's initial command to Abraham in Genesis 12 is to "go from your country and your kindred" (Genesis 12:1 ESV). God is explicit that Abraham not remain with his own people. The first command God gives to the first biblical patriarch actively encourages mixing with an ethnically diverse group of people who are not "kin" to Abraham. Theologian Thomas C. Oden pointed out,

> Cut Africa out of the Bible and Christian memory, and you have misplaced many pivotal scenes of salvation history. It is the story of the children of Abraham in Africa; Joseph in Africa; Moses in Africa; Mary, Joseph and Jesus in Africa; and shortly thereafter Mark, and Perpetua and Athanasius and Augustine in Africa.

The importance God places on creating a world with a plurality of ethnicities is never more present than in the book of Ruth. Here, a woman from the kingdom of Moab (today's Jordan) marries a man from the kingdom of Judah (today's Israel). Shortly thereafter, Ruth's husband dies. Ruth then travels to Bethlehem in Judah to work as a field hand for a man named Boaz, another Judean. The two eventually fall in love in a spectacular scene on a threshing floor and then marry. What is remarkable about the book is that it features not one but *two* instances of a mixed ethnic marriage where a Moabite woman marries a Judean man. But the happily-ever-after does not end there. Ruth, the Moabite woman, and Boaz, the Judean, eventually have a son they name Obed. By the book's end, we find out that Obed became the grandfather of King David. As it is written in the Gospels, Jesus is a descendant of King David. This means that the Son of God is born of a mixed ethnicity.

Yet, despite the Bible featuring mostly people of color and the Lord's frequent proclamations to encourage ethnic diversity, many today still imagine biblical Christians as mostly Europeans. The apostle Paul says that for the sake of spreading the gospel, he has "become all things to all people." If Christianity can be all things to all people, why then is whiteness treated as a universal biblical concept?

EARLY CHRISTIANS AND EUROPEAN RULE

Modern Christian history is ubiquitously associated with the European ruling class, but that has not always been the case. At its inception, Christianity was at odds with the Roman Empire. The late first century and early second century Roman ruling class and political elite were highly suspicious of the faith. They were offended that there were people who refused to worship Roman gods. Even worse, there were Europeans who abandoned their gods to follow the Jewish rabbi named Jesus.

There are numerous historical instances in which those among the Roman cultural elite saw Christianity similarly to the way many see it today. As one scholar puts it, they believed that Christianity was "a depraved, excessive, contagious, pernicious, new, and mischievous superstition. *Religion*, to put it bluntly, was what aristocratic Romans did; *superstition* was what others did—especially those unseemly types from regions east of Italy." Pliny the Younger, an early, second-century Roman governor, was so confused with the rise of Christianity in his region that he wrote an emergency dispatch to the Emperor Trajan. He explained that a number of Christians were brought before him. While the initial allegations are unclear, Pliny arbitrarily leveraged charges against Christians for their faith. He challenged them to deny Jesus. Some did, and their lives were spared. But others relentlessly held to their faith in Jesus, and Pliny executed them. The Roman governor was terrified by their bold Christian faith. He later wrote to the emperor, "This positiveness and inflexible obstinacy deserved to be punished." All of Rome grew nervous because the more the Romans persecuted Christians, the more the faith spread.

The Romans adopted a don't ask-don't-tell policy toward Christians. In his response to the governor, Trajan tells Pliny to punish Christians when their faith becomes apparent, but to refrain from seeking them out. For a while, Christianity remained a thorn in the side of the European ruling elite. There were intermittent periods of persecution and slaughter of Christians. But in AD 312, everything changed.

Constantine became the emperor of Rome. By that time, Rome began to splinter under mounting pressure of state-sanctioned paganism and illegal Christianity. Finally, when Constantine's own mother converted to the faith, the emperor saw the light. Constantine became the first Roman emperor to convert to Christianity.

WHEN EUROPEANS BECAME CHRISTIANS

In 313, Emperor Constantine officially legalized Christianity. By 380, Christianity became the official state religion of the Roman Empire. Over a span of about three hundred years, Christianity went from being an outlawed religion to the official religion of the same empire that had crucified Jesus. Christians went from the slaughter pens and torture chambers to ascendance of leadership roles in Rome.

For Rome to adopt Christianity as the state religion certainly sent shockwaves through the world. From Africa to Palestine to Rome, Christianity had a profound effect on faith formation, Roman traditions, and customs. An influential North African bishop named Augustine of Hippo wrote heavily influential works that offered a road map for how Christianity should shape the new political and societal frontier in the coming years. Slowly, the distinction diminished between what was culturally Roman and what was Christian.

By the fifth century, the Roman Empire collapsed at the hands of a loose collection of pagan Germanic tribes called the Goths.

The fall of the Roman Empire gave way to the long period of political instability known as the Middle Ages. There was no longer a Roman Empire, but Christianity remained a dominant political and cultural force throughout Europe.

Western and Eastern Europe parted ways and became a collection of warring states with everchanging borders. Without a strong centralized Roman rulership to bind kingdoms together, Europe experienced a power vacuum.

HOW A DARK-SKINNED FAITH BECAME WHITE

During the Middle Ages, the Church assumed political leadership. Catholic bishops and the pope became local governors and rulers of towns. Bishops became local government officials in charge of administering justice, running the markets, and making treaties with other towns. As Christian leaders took on key political roles in the Middle Ages, Christianity became the vessel for preserving Roman culture. Once the Roman Empire fell to the Goths, Roman traditions were in danger of disappearing. The arts, letters, and culture of Rome, which had flourished only a few hundred years earlier, were in danger of being lost without a centralized power to preserve them. The political, cultural, and religious realms were never entirely separate to begin with. But after the fall of Rome and the rise of Christians as state leaders, the marriage boundaries between the three became even more murky.

Only three hundred years earlier, Roman governors were calling Christianity a "superstition." Now, Christianity and Christian politicians were tasked with preserving Roman culture, music, art, and writing in the face of the uncivilized barbarian Goths who had burned down the empire. And it was in this moment—the dawn of the Middle Ages—that Christianity became seen as *progressive*. It sounds kind of backwards, doesn't it?

At this pivotal moment, Christianity defined itself in terms of what *it was not*. If the pagan Germanic Goths were backwards, uncivilized, and barbaric savages, then Christians were refined, civilized, and cultured. From a superstition formed in a backwater town into the paragon of defense against uncivilized barbarians, Christianity transformed from a backwards superstition to a progressive power by using the Goths and the sack of Rome as a backdrop for defining itself. European culture and Christianity fused; Christianity took a great leap forward. It may be argued, however, that the fusion of Christianity with Western society produced a religion that veered away from the teachings of Jesus and his disciples. The new religion that emerged kept Christianity as its name but substituted fidelity to Jesus for Western imperialism.

THE WHITE JESUS OF HOLLYWOOD

Moreover, ideological framing of Christianity as a white religion may be traced back as far as the fall of the Roman Empire, but it has remained in full throttle in North America during the nineteenth and twentieth centuries. The history of how heroic characters of the Bible—including Jesus and his apostles—became blond-haired, blue-eyed white men is long and complex. There is not enough space in this chapter to peel back all of the historical layers, but some key historical nuggets are worth covering to support the topic of this chapter.

The white Jesus in American Christianity emerged in the early nineteenth century. There were rising tensions between abolitionists and slaveholders. Each group dug their heels into biblical interpretations that lent authority to their respective

> To be more like Jesus meant to think, act, and even try to look white.

political cause. Particularly, slaveholders deployed images of a white Jesus, not only as a defense for enslaving people of color but also as an icon of achievement to which nonwhite minorities should aspire. To be more like Jesus meant to think, act, and even try to look white. Slaveholders lorded over their slaves, perpetuating the colonization of their minds just as much as oppressing them sociopolitically. As the Protestant religious revival known as the Second Great Awakening swept across America in the 1800s, the production of religious icons grew exponentially. White America needed a white Jesus with whom to identify and affirm its supremacy during slavery and later during the Jim Crow era. Historians Edward Blum and Paul Harvey note,

> Whether through tracts, Sunday school cards, or church art or on television and in movies, visual depictions of Christ lodged the idea of his whiteness deep within cultural conventions and individual psyches. . . . The goal of the pictures was to teach Christianity, but an unintended consequence was to create an often-unspoken belief that Jesus was white.

The widespread portrayal of a white Jesus became a staple in the American religious imagination so much so that many black Christians imagined Jesus as white. There was just no way Jesus was a man of color. Anything worth aspiring to, believing in, and worshiping was obviously white. We all know the look: long brown hair, mid-length beard, blue eyes, and pale, fair skin. This image of Jesus came from Hollywood in the 1920s, and despite an abundance of historical evidence to the contrary, it has remained part of the Hollywood production of biblical stories well into the twenty-first century. The question we must ask is, why?

The early 1900s represented a significant turning point in American history. Wall Street was breaking records daily and the Great Depression hit not long after. Black people began migrating from the South to the North, starting businesses and black centers of arts, letters, and culture in places such as Harlem and Black Wall Street in Tulsa, Oklahoma, and more. The Klan that originated in the late 1800s had been re-formed in the South and was terrorizing black people, their families, and their businesses. Lest we forget, they did it all in the name of Jesus. Members of the KKK included deacons, so-called

Christian leaders, and Bible-toting Christians. They burned crosses as a symbol of their Christian claims. All the while, the tiny agricultural village of Hollywood became an overnight filmmaking boomtown.

In the backlots of MGM and Warner Brothers, directors and producers were hard at work turning biblical stories into movie productions. They cast all white actors to play Moses, Jesus, God, and most of the rest of the biblical characters. Only antagonists like the Egyptians and marginal supporting characters such as Simon of Cyrene were portrayed as darker-skinned people.

Starting in the 1920s, Hollywood gave the world its first moving picture of Jesus in Cecil DeMille's *The King of Kings*. The opening fades from black into Jesus' white face looking back at viewers—the embodiment of a white savior, complete with a halo around his head. When DeMille filmed the crucifixion scenes, he enlisted the help of D. W. Griffith, the producer of *Birth of a Nation*, which is a film heroically detailing the Ku Klux Klan. Upon the film's release, it was positively reviewed as being similar in style to Griffith's *Birth of a Nation*, not least of all because the film's heroes were all white. Though some called *The King of Kings* "the most important picture ever made," others deplored it for its lack of an authentic looking Jesus. Jesus, one reviewer noted, was *not white enough*. For some, the image of Jesus in the movie needed to be white with blond hair and blue eyes.

JESUS IN THE BOOKS

Around the same time as the release of *The King of Kings*, author Upton Sinclair wrote a short book called *They Call Me Carpenter: A Tale of the Second Coming*. In the story, a young man named Billy cruises around Hollywood and decides to see a movie. At the theater, he is attacked by an angry mob and forced to seek shelter inside of a church. Once inside, he sees a stained-glass window: "You know, of course, the sort of figures they have in those windows; a man in long robes, white, with purple and gold; with a brown beard, and a gentle, sad face, and a halo of light about the head."

Then, suddenly, the figure walks out of the window. Jesus, or Carpenter (as he liked to be called), is ready to hit the town with Billy. In order to make sure none of the church folk notice he is missing, Jesus grabs a portrait of a white bank manager to hang in his place thinking no one would notice the difference. Immediately afterwards, Jesus gets swept up into the movie business as a pushy filmmaker becomes obsessed with his face and wants desperately to put him into "propaganda films fer de churches." To the film-maker's dismay, Jesus turns him down to heal the sick and feed the hungry around Los Angeles—a practice that does not sit too well with the aristocracy, who quickly commission a mob to lynch Jesus.

Billy, distraught by the thought of losing his friend, remembers seeing *Birth of a Nation* and hires his own mob to defend Jesus. In the story, Billy hires all the extras from D. W. Griffith's film to dress in the KKK's robes and rally around Jesus to protect him. While Billy's plan works, Jesus has had enough and exclaims, "Let me go back where I was, where I do not see, where I do not hear, where I do not think! Let me go back to the church!" Jesus rushes back to the window that he walked out of and disappears.

THE PUSHBACK AND CONSEQUENCE

Several things are remarkable about Upton Sinclair's fiction. As early as 1922, it was quite ubiquitous in the United States for Jesus to be found as a white icon. He had been so enculturated into white America's social and political agenda that a mob of Klansmen agreed to defend him from an entirely different angry mob. In the story, the Klansmen are on Jesus' side! This imagery is a social painting of the Klansmen as good guys and implies theologically that Jesus supports the KKK's agenda. Also, Jesus replaces his own portrait with that of a white banker. Notice that the two of them look identical!

A deeper social critical analysis reveals that during the horror of the Jim Crow era, as the KKK attacked, beat, drowned, and hung people of color left and right and hated the Jews, Sinclair's short story shows that a large number of Christians consented to these acts as if it were what God wanted. While Sinclair's novel is fiction, the religious art of a white Jesus is not something merely fictional. It was common in American churches and, yes, in many black churches too.

Although there was pervasive hostility against people of color, there arose significant pushback from Native American and black communities. They fought against the idea that the white supremacists' agenda was God's agenda and that biblical heroes were all white. In fact, the uncritical assimilation to the image of a white Jesus being posted in many black churches infuriated a few radical black leaders such as Elijah Muhammad of the Nation of Islam and F. S. Cherry, also known as Prophet Cherry, who launched a campaign against images of a white biblical figures during the same time Sinclair wrote his story.

Prophet Cherry, founder of the Church of the Living God and key creator of the Black Israelites movement, was convinced that because the majority of the people in the Bible were from an Afro-Asiatic context, "God and biblical figures such as Adam, Eve, and Jesus were physically black." Cherry made it his goal to strip churches of their white art. While preaching in a black church, he once pointed to a portrait of white Jesus and said, "I'll give anybody one thousand dollars tomorrow night who can tell me who the hell that is!"

The white Bible of the 1920s and 1930s had lasting and damaging psychological consequences for young African Americans. Blum and Harvey report a study from then-head of Howard University's sociology department, E. Franklin Frazier, that highlights the malignancy of beliefs that the Bible is composed of only white people. Frazier conducted a study asking numerous young African Americans "Is God a White Man?" Their answers were startling.

One twenty-one-year-old responded, "I've never heard of him being a Negro so he must have been a white man. People would think you were crazy if you told them he was a Negro, especially white people." Another nineteen-year-old added, "Negro or white, by the time white people got through, they made him white, too." And finally, a college freshman remarked, "All the pictures I've seen, he was a white man. If by any chance he was anything else, the white people have taken great pains to make him a white man throughout these many, many years."

Indeed, Hollywood did and has continued over the past twenty years to portray biblical characters as white despite overwhelming historical evidence that Jesus probably had dark, olive skin. By 2005, there were six big-budget Hollywood films about Jesus, all featuring a white Jesus and friends. And with foreign markets accounting for over 60 percent of Hollywood's box office, white Jesus reached a lot of nonwhite Christians. Even well into 2019, Hollywood continued to produce images of a Caucasian Bible. Most notably these productions include the History Channel's *Jesus: His Life* and Darren Aronofsky's *Noah*, each featuring ahistorical fair-skinned leads for Jesus and Noah respectively.

Hollywood's project of bringing a white Bible to the big screen highlights the hold that a white Christian imagination has on America's idea of the color of the Bible. While Sinclair's short story details the absurdity of an Aryan Jesus, Frazier's study nonetheless shows how deeply entrenched it is in the minds of young African Americans.

The early fusion between European culture and Christianity paired with the influence from Hollywood thoroughly established that everyone from the Hebrew Bible to the New Testament was white. Despite early vocal critiques over the abundant display of white

> **Despite early vocal critiques over the abundant display of white biblical figures in books, movies, and churches, the historical inaccuracy of a white Bible has proved remarkably difficult to overturn.**

biblical figures in books, movies, and churches, the historical inaccuracy of a white Bible has proved remarkably difficult to overturn.

LIVING IT OUT

Race as we know it today did not exist in biblical times. The way history has contorted biblical characters to support European imperialistic agendas is a social construct. To reimagine the original diversity in Scripture and Christianity, we must first problematize this socially manufactured concept of race. It has far too long imposed itself upon biblical history and the origins of the faith. Secondly, the Bible is chock full of ethnic and cultural diversity.

An excavation of biblical history reveals that from Genesis to Revelation, God has affirmed people from the kaleidoscope of national, cultural, and social locations. History also confirms that Christianity was born out of the context of marginalized descendants of Abraham in first-century Palestine with a clear mission of drawing all of humanity onto equal footing as God's people. Christians must renew their commitment to God's agenda and abandon distorted images and claims on a racialized faith. Racialization runs interference with God's global agenda of love. Social stratification of any kind is an insult of God's creative genius.

CHAPTER SEVEN

THE GENESIS CURSE?

Many have found within [the Bible's] pages justifications for
slavery, abuse of African-Americans and segregation.

KARL GIBERSON

At a recent Bible study, someone commented that black people
have reason to thank God for slavery because he used slavery
to deliver black people from the savagery of Africa and introduce
them to Jesus. The comment would be funny if it were not so pathetic!
Ironically, this was not the first time I heard such a perspective. All
over the country—in pews, communities, and universities—a similar
perspective makes its way into the race conversation. It's an idea
deeply rooted in the assumption that black people have been cursed
since the times we read about in Genesis.

For centuries, mainstream Christianity has portrayed the biblical
origins of the world as European. Theologian Keith Augustus
Burton notes that most illustrated biblical books published in the
1980s and 1990s depict Adam, Eve, and the angels as Scandinavian.
Cecil B. DeMille's *The Ten Commandments*, released in 1956, is the
sixth highest grossing film in the United States and Canada. Beyond
the theater, the VHS, DVD, and Netflix versions of the movie have
become a staple in Christian homes, youth groups, churches, and
schools. While the movie was well-done and seeks to preserve the
Old Testament's narrative of the Ten Commandments, there are
several subliminal messages within. For example, God's people look

European, they speak English with a European accent, and people of color are either God's enemies or slaves.

Similarly, Mel Gibson's film *The Passion of the Christ* smashed the box office in 2004. Both Christians and non-Christians have noted its fidelity to the biblical narrative, but Gibson added a language dynamic suggesting to viewers that the language of the New Testament was not English but Jewish, Palestinian, Aramaic, Latin, and Hebrew. While this gets us closer to the Middle Eastern context in which the story took place, there remains much to ponder. For example, the Greco-Roman symbolic world was prominent. Jesus was a Jew but spoke common Greek; it was called *koinē* Greek, a vernacular comparable to Ebonics among Southern blacks in the English speaking world today. Most Palestinian Jews spoke *koinē*, or the common language, in the first century. Also, DeMille's *The Ten Commandments* and Gibson's *The Passion of the Christ* contain subliminal messages that have Western cultural implications, including that the heroes in both films look European. This implies (in Gibson's film) that while the New Testament heroes may have spoken a different language, they were still white.

Charlton Heston played Moses in *The Ten Commandments* and Jim Caviezel portrayed Jesus in *The Passion of the Christ*. White actors playing biblical heroes only reinforce white religious heroism and domination over nonwhites. Both movies sustain the religious assumption passed down since colonial Christianity that the Bible is full of white people with a few people of color representing evildoers, like the Egyptians in *The Ten Commandments* or Simon of Cyrene portrayed by Jarreth J. Merz in *The Passion of the Christ*. The pervasive white heroism against black evilness and servitude has painted the canvas of biblical history such that many black Christians have adopted its assumptions.

Furthermore, the movies reflect Western imperial ambition rather than the historically accurate cultural world of the Bible. From Genesis to Revelation, the majority of the people in the Bible are from an Afro-Asiatic context with a range of brown skin, thick and thin lips, broad and slender noses, tall and fat structures, and so on. There are indeed people of a European descent in the New Testament, but they have a much less prominent presence than Hollywood would have us believe.

I can't count the many times black people have asked me questions like, "Doc, did Moses marry a black woman?" "Was Simon of Cyrene black?" "Wasn't the Ethiopian eunuch black?" My short answer is "Yes, yes, and yes!" My longer answer is in response to the troubling reality that many people of color ask such questions because they want to identify with who they have been made to believe are a few "good" people of color in the Bible. These include Moses' Cushite wife (Numbers 12:1); Simon of Cyrene, who helped Jesus carry his cross (Matthew 27:32; Mark 15:21; Luke 23:26); and the Ethiopian eunuch (Acts 8:27), who Phillip baptized. It makes sense to ask about the black people in the Bible we consider "good" ones.

It is mindboggling how Western society formed the notion that black people are the product of a divine curse. For centuries, the United States in particular has told Bible stories that assume the majority of the people in the Bible are white. The not-so-subtle agenda advances the notion that white ways of thinking and doing are right and blessed because white people are the chosen ones. People of color are not to be trusted because they are cursed and fated to serve white people. These sentiments undergirded colonialism, slavery, and Jim Crow laws. Yet the "white is right" propaganda was not limited to the Americas. It permeated Asia and Africa as an international force.

THE "CURSE" OF BLACKNESS?

For centuries, white supremacy shaped biblical interpretive lenses. It was widely believed that blackness is a curse leaving black people socialized within a negative self-conscious state. In the ancient

Greco-Roman world, to be black meant to have inferior intelligence, so much so that Alexandria, a city in Egypt famous for learning, was talked about as separate from Africa. The Romans called it *Alexandria ad Aegyptum*, meaning "Alexandria near Egypt," as opposed to Alexandria *in* Egypt.

Associating wisdom with blackness was dangerous. Even the three wise men were used to socialize black people into an inferior mind. Following Jesus' birth three kings from different countries come to deliver gifts to the newborn child. Two of the kings are white while the other, Gaspar, is a black Ethiopian. As early as the seventh century CE the three kings became tools to symbolize white supremacy. One German archbishop declared that the two white kings symbolized a mature faith while Gaspar symbolized Africa "where the faith was the youngest." Thus, African cultures became canonized "as the youngest, rudimentary" and in need of white Eurocentric education. It's hard to read today's racial prejudice into the ancient world, but skin color *did* matter. The ancient Greeks and Romans made distinctions between lighter Africans (*fusci*) and darker Africans (*nigerrimi*). And those colors easily dictated where one fell on a social scale between slave and freedman.

> Blackness in the ancient world was associated with rudimentary thinking and youthful ignorance. In our more recent history, blackness was seen as disease that could be caught.

Blackness in the ancient world was associated with rudimentary thinking and youthful ignorance. In our more recent history, blackness was seen as disease that could be caught. For instance, under Jim Crow's segregation, not only was it illegal for black people to drink out of the same water fountains as white people, whites would go so far as to wash their hands after touching a black person. As noted above, Alexandria had to be kept separate from the rest of Africa or it could contaminate the city's knowledge. G. Elliot Smith, who conducted the first archaeological study of southern Egypt, remarked, "The smallest infusion of Negro blood immediately manifests itself in a dulling of initiative and a 'drag' on the further development of the arts of civilization."

Not only did the "curse" of blackness frame historical views among whites, but also the overwhelming Western force of ideas cultivated inferiority among blacks. The rationale that blackness is a curse fed into assumptions as recent as the 1970s that blacks are unintelligent and less capable of learning than whites. Samuel G. Morton, the founder of paleontology, studied human skulls to spot racial differences in intelligence. He broke all the world's races down into five categories, including Ethiopians—a catchall term for all black people.

The curse of Cain. Colonial Christianity drilled down on the idea that blackness is a curse and that black people experienced their greatest blessing in European civilization. It pointed to Eurocentrism as the true nature of God's people. The message was coupled with a few different myths, one of which was that dark-skinned people are descendants of Cain.

In 2019, I was guest lecturer at a leadership conference in Luanda, Angola. While there, my host took me to the Slave Museum. The first black slaves that were shipped to the New World came from Angola. The so-called Portuguese Empire saw themselves as the next great imperium after the fall of Rome. In their oceanic explorations, the Portuguese landed in Africa. They were fascinated with Africa's richness of gold and diamonds. They insisted on taking the land from the natives. The Portuguese were also struck by the work ethic and agricultural innovation they observed among the Africans. So, they did not want to kill them off. They saw the people as a commodity along with the wealth the land possessed. They determined to take the land and sell the people as slaves in lands that could benefit from their agricultural genius. Along the west coast,

Portuguese merchants settled in both Guinea and Angola. Along the east coast, they settled in Mozambique and near the Zambezi river. They claimed that they relied on God, and they used their guns to subjugate African natives to slavery.

I was stunned to learn that the Portuguese conjured up the idea that just as Adam's son Cain was cursed to be a nomad in the land, Africans lived as undeserving vagabonds in the beautiful lands of Africa. Portuguese slave traders built their homes on the Atlantic coast of Angola with churches attached to their homes. They captured Africans and taught them that they were descendants of Cain, meaning they were cursed people who could only gain redemption through baptism into the Christian faith. This message also carried the caveat that Africans would find the fullness of their redemption in Christ through slavery in the New World.

The Portuguese Catholic colonizers and slave traders had millions of Africans baptized and then chained them together and escorted them to the shores of the Atlantic Ocean to board slave ships. They shipped some of them off to Brazil and sold others to the English in the colonies of the New World that would later become known as New York and Virginia. Of course, the British followed suit in colonizing Western African countries such as Gambia, Ghana, Nigeria, Southern Cameroon, and Sierra Leone, where they also captured natives and sold them as slaves to the Americas.

From the sixteenth century until 1860, slave traders used God and guns to subjugate Africans to slave brutality. They brainwashed slaves with scriptural explanations that emphasized African inferiority based on the curse of their so-called Genesis ancestors. The colonizers advertently fed their own superiority and pockets at the expense of oppressing the African people with their interpretations of the Bible. They attacked and killed those who refused to surrender. Although the natives were not necessarily deceived into thinking they were really cursed, they were not prepared to battle as effectively as they wanted because the Europeans fought with guns. Africans had never even seen guns before.

The curse of Ham. In 2016, I visited the tiny Slave Museum in the city of Calabar in Cross River State of Nigeria. It was interesting to hear the slave narrative from the Nigerian perspective. Many of the lessons were similar to the ones I learned in Angola. One striking difference was another European religious rationale for slavery. It was the myth that dark-skinned people are all the "cursed" sons of Ham. This was actually the justification for slavery I had heard since I was a child. The myth I heard in Angola about Cain's descendants was new to me.

Concerning the myth of the "curse of Ham," Keith A. Burton says,

> The myth has become so common that many have placed the text about the "curse of Ham" in their own imaginative Bibles next to verses like "cleanliness is next to godliness" or "God helps those who help themselves." Armed with a cadre of textual misinterpretations, allegations of a cursed race have been used to subjugate the peoples of Africa and other dark-skinned people for over a millennia.

Over the past fifty years, black scholars have made a point of getting to the bottom of this claim. It finds its biblical source in the story of Ham, who disrespected his father Noah. As a result of his disrespect, the belief is that God cursed his seed to be black. Let's take a closer look at this claim with the following questions in mind:

- Is there a biblical curse on black people?
- Does the Bible really say that black people are cursed? Or is this simply an interpretive claim?

After the flood, Noah and his sons began populating the earth. While the Bible does not explicitly state the color of Noah's skin, the names of his children are good indicators of their skin color as well as his own. While Japheth means "bright, fair, or very light,"

Shem means "brownish or dusky," and Ham is Hebrew for "hot, burnt, dark." In Genesis 9:25, Noah said, "Cursed be Canaan; a servant of servants he shall be to his brethren." The curse was not on Ham, the father of all dark-skinned descendants, but on the one son, Canaan. Genesis 9:18-25 has been popularly interpreted as justification of the oppression and enslavement of black people because of the alleged curse of Ham. Theologian Robert Hood notes, "The formation of American culture cannot be understood without Ham's children in the very formation and development of America's character." The Scripture reads,

> The sons of Noah who came out of the ark were Shem, Ham and Japheth. (Ham was the father of Canaan.) These were the three sons of Noah, and from them came the people who were scattered over the whole earth.
>
> Noah, a man of the soil, proceeded to plant a vineyard. When he drank some of its wine, he became drunk and lay uncovered inside his tent. Ham, the father of Canaan, saw his father naked and told his two brothers outside. But Shem and Japheth took a garment and laid it across their shoulders; then they walked in backward and covered their father's naked body. Their faces were turned the other way so that they would not see their father naked. When Noah awoke from his wine and found out what his youngest son had done to him, he said,
>
> "Cursed be Canaan!
> The lowest of slaves
> will he be to his brothers." (Genesis 9:19-25)

Colonialists read the "curse of Canaan" as a curse upon all of Ham's children. In any case, of Ham's four children—Cush, Misrayim, Put, and Canaan—Noah only pronounced the curse on Canaan. The colonists mislabeled the curse of Canaan as the curse of Ham. For example, a Methodist cleric in Tennessee stated a popular opinion at the time:

Japheth alone received Christianity which Shem rejected as the messenger of light, and then sunk again to slumber through ages dark with dismal dreams. . . . Providence lifted the veil and showed him America, the birthright of Shem, and bade him inherit and enter, possess and improve. He gave him the ancient commission to coerce the race of Ham to bear its part of tribute by tilling the soil and subduing the earth.

Another example is Frederick Dalcho, who was a South Carolina minister that argued in his sermon, "The declaration of the Fourth of July belongs exclusively to the white population of the United States. The American Revolution was a family quarrel among whites. In this the Negroes had no concern, their condition remained, and must remain, unchanged."

"Their condition" no doubt refers to their divinely given inferiority. As a child of Ham, one is always enslaved. Dalcho is far from alone. Episcopal Bishop John Hopkins said in 1863,

Where, then, I ask, did the authors of the *Declaration of Independence* find their warrant for such a statement ["all men are created equal" and "endowed with certain unalienable rights"]? . . . To estimate aright the vast diversity among the races of mankind, we may begin with our own, the highly privileged Anglo-Saxon, which now stands at the head, although our ancestors were heathen barbarians only two thousand years ago. From this we may go down the descending scale through the Turks . . . the Abyssinians, the Africans, and how is it possible to imagine that God has made them all equal! . . . The facts rather establish the very contrary.

Hopkins, like Morton before him, classifies the world races in a hierarchy. He puts what he calls the South's "posterity of Ham" at the bottom, as chosen by God.

Hood correctly explains, "The Ham legend has been a part of the mythic structure about blackness and inferiority of blacks that comes up again and again in Western thought." And that mythic structure especially rears its ugly head in American churches where God's Word has been repeatedly evoked to maintain the curse of Ham narrative.

AFRICANS IN THE LAND OF KUSH, NOT CANAAN

Based on Genesis 10, Kush and Misrayim were likely ancestors of many African descendants. Thus, any assumption that Africans are afflicted by the curse of Canaan is a misapplied conclusion. Canaanites did not migrate to the continent of Africa. Kush migrated to Africa. The continent of Africa was not a product of the Curse of Canaan.

The kingdoms of Kush included that of the modern nations of Sudan, Eritrea, Djibouti, and Ethiopia. In biblical times, Nimrod, a son of Ethiopia, established Babylon, Erech, Akkad, Calneh, and Assyria (Genesis 10:8-11). His region of influence covered areas of modern day Iraq, Jordan, and parts of Syria. Nimrod's territory also overlapped areas occupied by Shem's descendants, including Abraham. This means that Cush's descendants were closely aligned with Shem's descendants early on. In fact, Scripture credits Nimrod as a mighty warrior. He led one of the earliest civilizations with unmatched technological advancements. The Tower of Babel was his greatest failure. According to the Genesis account, God stopped Nimrod's genius because he used it to make a name for himself rather than to glorify God.

Next, Ham's son Misrayim features prominently throughout biblical history as well. According to the Table of Nations in Genesis 10, Misrayim had oversight in the modern territories of Algeria, Tunisia, Morocco, and Libya, as well as the island of Crete in the Mediterranean. Scholars have noted a historical misalignment between territory and kingdom. However, it remains clear that Misrayim's descendants occupied vast measures of the aforementioned regions.

Of the remaining sons of Ham, Canaan remains the most prominent in Scripture while very little evidence exists to trace Put's descendants. However, Canaan's territory is that which God promised to Shem's descendants—the children of Israel. While it is not entirely clear as to whether the curse of Canaan is achieved when the Israelites possess their land, one may conjecture this to be the case. Yet, it is even clearer that the curse had nothing to do with the other descendants of Ham who went on to populate much of Africa.

Hood explains that part of the confusion about this curse may arise from the fact that "Ethiopia has been on a racial and ethnic pendulum." He adds that Ethiopia has been subject to the whims of white American anthropologists and archaeologists. White American and European academics commonly recast Ethiopia into whatever mold fit their agendas. For example, Hood notes that there have

> **The so-called curse of Ham simply never existed. It is the figment of racist imagination to subjugate blacks to an inferior status based on their blackness.**

been times when they described Ethiopian (Kushite) rulers as Caucasian when speaking of early influential civilizations for the rest of sub-Saharan Africa. However, the same kings were later called black in the context of speaking about their inferior achievements in relation to ancient Egypt. Stated differently, black people were cursed because of Ham, except for the ones who were successful. The so-called curse of Ham simply never existed. It is the figment of racist imagination to subjugate blacks to an inferior status based on their blackness. And, the curse of Canaan was not eternal, but a prophetic proclamation forecasting the interrelationships between Canaan's descendants and the descendants of the rest of the family.

LIVING IT OUT

Few people seem to understand that there is a broad representation of cultural diversity throughout the Bible. The continent of Africa and its people are prominently featured. Black people have lived in the shadows of this fact. Suppressing this fact has worked for mainstream society and successfully kept black people from their sacred presence in the origins of early Christian history.

With the rise of Black nationalist groups like the Black Israelites, the Nation of Islam, and other spontaneous movements, the minds of many young people hang in the balance. Are we cursed or not? If the Bible says we are, then it is not on black people's side. Why would I trust a Bible that says I'm cursed? And if that is not the case, then what is the truth? When our eyes are opened to the ideological backdrop that has, in many, ways colonized the Christian mind to think that black is cursed, we locate the vastness of human affirmation in Scripture. Until then, we miss significant liberation to think about the faith of Christ as freedom to be who God made us and not who we feel compelled to try to be like. God loves you and me for who we are. You are not cursed. You are loved, wanted, and blessed in Christ!

PART THREE

A FAITH THAT CARES

ABOUT PEOPLE FROM

DIFFERENT CULTURES

CHAPTER EIGHT

READING THE NEW TESTAMENT
THROUGH DARK LENSES

*The biblical role of non-Europeans in general and blacks in particular
has . . . been trivialized and left in the margins, as has their role
in salvation history subsequent to the redaction of the Bible.*

CAIN HOPE FELDER

In an increasingly diverse world, we must read Scripture for its
affirmation of every human being—from the socially elite to
dwellers in the world's slums; from the powerful to the distressed;
from refugees to undocumented immigrants in pursuit of political
asylum; from the most erudite to the illiterate; and even the hus-
tlers on the corner. Every human being is invited to have a relationship with Jesus. Just as Europeans encountered a white Jesus,
Latinos, Indian people in Africa, and others must bring their
sociocultural locations to bear on biblical interpretation. This is
what the incarnation is all about. God comes among us in God's
Son, Jesus Christ, to take up residence in our sociocultural locations (John 1:14).

In Matthew 1:23, God says, "The virgin will conceive and give
birth to a son, and they will call him Immanuel" (which in Hebrew
means "God with us"). When we read Scripture through the "God
with us" lens, we encounter the incarnated Christ amid all of

God's people to help, heal, and give hope. Crystal Valentine, an African American poet, succinctly offers a contemporary interpretation of the incarnation in a passionate response to Megyn Kelly's disastrous claim that Jesus is white. In Valentine's piece titled, "And the News Reporter Says Jesus Is White," she says in expressive words,

How can she say Jesus was a white man when he died the
    Blackest way possible?
With his hands up
With his mother watching
Crying at his feet

Her words conjure images of unarmed black men murdered in the streets, juxtaposed with the crucifixion of Jesus. By highlighting the commonality of experience, she frames the blackness of Jesus. It's a different notion of blackness than those who claim that Jesus was of black heritage in attempt to find identity with him. Instead, she highlights what I'll call an "experiential heritage." Christ's experience of suffering and humiliation at the hands of oppressive (governmental) powers allows the oppressed and suffering of this world to identity with him. In the American context, this is true for many people in the African American community. Netflix commentator Killer Mike argues that we need a black messiah. When properly understood, Jesus is a black messiah—that is, Jesus is intimately present in black, white, brown, and all people's suffering.

CHRIST'S MISSION STATEMENT

Identity and representation are central concerns for the majority of people when it comes to embracing faith. In light of this reality, the image of Jesus as a blonde-haired, blue-eyed European that has come to dominate the public imagination is a great tragedy. It's tempting to dismiss such a development as merely a negligent historical inaccuracy but doing so would ignore the fact that this image of Jesus is the result of Western Europeans remaking God in their own image. Ultimately, we must engage with the Jesus of Scripture, not his misrepresentations propagated through media and popular culture. Unfortunately, few people have sought out this Jesus. Most have come to base their understanding of Jesus on secondhand information. As a result, the dominant culture in the West has maintained the authoritative voice on the appearance, character, and experience of Jesus, allowing him to be misrepresented and reduced to a mere icon, the radical nature of his life and teachings mostly ignored. With this misrepresentation in mind, many disillusioned black millennials ask, "How can I identify with this Jesus?" The quickest rebuttal is to ask, "Who does Jesus identify with?" and seek the answer in Scripture. The Gospel of Luke offers an answer that couldn't be any clearer. The narrative in 4:18-19 presents Jesus right before he begins his ministry marking his first public declaration. Picture a well-known figure or politician making an impromptu announcement that they are running for president. The only difference is that up until this point Jesus was obscure and unknown. According to Luke, Jesus stands up in the synagogue and declares:

> The Spirit of the Lord is upon me,
>> because he has anointed me
>>> to proclaim good news to the poor.
> He has sent me to proclaim liberty to the captives
>> and recovery of sight to the blind,
>>> to set at liberty those who are oppressed,
> to proclaim the year of the Lord's favor.
>> (Luke 4:18-19 ESV)

This is a remarkable statement. In these verses, Jesus makes a public announcement that essentially doubles as a mission statement— one that lacks the characteristics of white Jesus as he's been popularized by dominant culture. Hence, we must ask ourselves, who is Jesus referencing? The poor, the captives, the blind, and the oppressed! Based on that observation, if we believe that the good news of Christ is relevant for today's generation, we must ask, who are the poor and oppressed of our age? With such a lens, we quickly see that the radical and liberative essence of Christ is closer to the experience of black America than many have been misled to believe. Undoubtedly, Christ's mission is a message of liberation—liberation from bondage with all of its ramifications within the human experience. Christ's bold confrontation of the oppressive realities plaguing humanity is a divine call to attention. To embrace Christ is to commit to his mission, which means that the oppressed see Christ intentionally pursuing them in their experience and the privileged embrace Christ among the oppressed.

If Christ himself identifies in a special way with the oppressed, then to identify with Christ is to identify with the oppressed as well. Through this framework, we see more clearly that the white-washing of Jesus and Christianity distorts his very essence. It has made Christ inaccessible to the very people that he prioritized. When we acknowledge the full extent of Christ's mission in the world, we recognize that any expression of Christianity that ignores or justifies the sorrowful conditions of the poor and disenfranchised is one that has lost its meaning.

Yet, the whitewashing of Jesus is only the tip of the iceberg. Beneath such imagery lies an interpretation of the Bible that centers the powerful and sidelines the oppressed. Jesus has been broadly removed from the culture of his day and replaced with a lens focused on Western culture and its white majority. To renounce "the white man's religion" then requires one to engage Jesus and read the New Testament with a different perspective, a view focused on the lives of the burdened, weak, and wearied. Christianity will not have any meaning or impact in the United States of America apart from doing so.

The blackness of Jesus from Valentine's poem connects to a long heritage of black spirituality on this continent. Enslaved Africans suffering under the brutality of the antebellum South found hope in Christ not because he was forced on them, but because they found familiarity in him. A faith that comforted and emboldened an enslaved people is the faith that we must rediscover. James Cone expresses this reality most clearly when he states,

> Until we can see the cross and the lynching tree together, until we can identify Christ with a "recrucified" black body hanging from a lynching tree, there can be no genuine understanding of Christian identity in America, and no deliverance from the brutal legacy of slavery and white supremacy.

The task before us is to learn how to discover Jesus afresh by reading the New Testament with a darker lens.

SEEING CHRIST IN COLOR

In the West, spirituality is generally thought of as a private and internal affair. Many have been indoctrinated to believe the Christian faith is only for the salvation of our souls and, as a result, we only engage Jesus in light of what he did on the cross for our benefit. Most churches talk about Christ's death and resurrection with his ministry relegated to the background. There is much more to Jesus' life and ministry. Without a doubt, Christ's death and resurrection are the central tenets of Christianity; however, if his death and resurrection are separated from his teaching and historical context, their meaning becomes distorted. Jesus' ministry cannot be overlooked if we are to engage the fullness of his revelation in the Scriptures. His ministry provides deep insight into the way in which God has chosen to redeem and restore humanity.

The first important detail in reading the New Testament is that God chose to be human. He took on flesh, became a man, and walked among us. This is a scandalous idea among the history of religious ideas. The incarnation is important for the oppressed because everyone has a body. The rich possess wealth, the academic have intellect, but they cannot escape the fact of their mortal bodies. In these bodies, we feel pain, experience hunger and thirst, and, ultimately, face death. Jacques Ellul explains the significance of this fact in this way, "God descends to humanity and joins us where we are. This is the opposite of the religious movement, in which people would like to ascend to where God is. Hence, we see a radical contradiction between all religions and the fundamental path of Revelation."

Far too often, we think of the goal of the Christian gospel as pulling us away from the human experience into the spiritual realm. But the incarnation of Christ points to something quite the opposite. The Son of God saw fit to become human—an act divinely affirming our humanity. As humans made in the image of God, we see Jesus Christ embrace our physical form. We don't worship God as an abstract idea, but by means of a savior, a king who exists in a human body forevermore. Hence, any ideology that seeks to devalue or subjugate the human body is an affront on God. The dehumanization of the black body is an insult to Christ himself who took on human flesh in order to redeem humanity—including our bodies. Slaveholder Christianity emphasizes the souls of select human beings but neglects their bodily oppression. Such a conception of Christianity is foreign to the New Testament, yet it continues to linger in today's Christian landscape. Many argue that oppression and injustice are inconsequential because God is more concerned with the souls of men. Martin Luther King Jr. highlighted this misguided spirituality when he wrote,

> In the midst of a mighty struggle to rid our nation of racial and economic injustice, I have heard so many ministers say, "those are social issues with which the gospel has no real concern," and I have watched so many churches commit themselves to a completely other-worldly religion which made a strange distinction between body and soul, the sacred and the secular.

For Dr. King, the insistence on creating a dichotomy between body and soul seemed aloof and not Christian.

THE HUMILITY OF JESUS

We are filled with illusions about what God looks like. Once, I received a call from a blocked number. Thinking it was my mentor, I eagerly answered only to discover it was someone else asking, "Why do people put this 400-year-old picture of God up in their churches and houses?" Taken aback by the question, I probed to understand what the person was really asking. Soon, it became clear that they were confused about Michelangelo's depiction of a white Jesus Christ made popular in many Western Christian circles for centuries. I explained to the anonymous caller that the picture was an artist's imagination at work and not an original depiction of Jesus. While I cannot get into Michelangelo's head to know exactly what he was thinking, it is safe to say that the picture of Jesus that he painted was a reflection of both his view of high reverence and personal relatability.

The caller wanted me to confirm that Jesus is also relatable to contemporary situations and the blight of the urban communities.

I explained to the man that the actual image of Jesus is not known today. There is no original photograph. But, a first-century carpenter's stepson who was born in a stinking stable with an animal's food trough as his crib was probably not a very lofty picture. The cute nativity scenes we set up at Christmastime romanticize a shocking reality. The savior came to the world in a non-elitist manner! In other words, God revealed God's self in the humblest way. The king of kings bypassed the grandeur of palaces to make his entrance into the world surrounded by animals. This should speak powerfully to uncelebrated and rejected people, those made to feel insignificant and unworthy. The Christian story reveals that God delights in dignifying the humble with his presence and humbling the proud and mighty. This should give us new perspective on the ghettos, inner cities, and struggling communities. These are all places near to God's heart. It may surprise you that these undesirable places and situations are also rich with divine revelation.

Jesus' background reveals something insightful for the black experience. Nazareth was a city of Galilee and the place of Jesus' upbringing. His background came burdened with prejudice. The Gospel of John records that Jesus received derision and scorn from those who learned of his hometown. Nathaniel, a would-be disciple remarks, "Can anything good come out of Nazareth?" (John 1:46 ESV). Supposedly, this was a common phrase of the day, as Nazareth was a small village of low reputation.

Discrimination and racial prejudice continue to hinder the flourishing of black people in America. Many black people are ashamed of their backgrounds, the black experience, and their culture. Research reveals that prospective employers are 36 percent less likely to call back candidates whose résumés feature African American names than those with culturally white European names. Black people in America face the same query everyday: "Can anything good come out of Tanisha or Daquan?" Black millennials are carrying the impact of deeply segregated communities and school systems. Black communities face severe systemic neglect and abuse. Many schools in urban black communities are under-resourced, leaving kids uninterested in education and with little vision for the future. "Can anything good come out of the hood?" is a question black youth have wrestled with throughout their experiences. Jesus empathizes with it. He walked the same road. Humble beginnings are not a thing of shame to God and we must emphasize this reality for the black millennials searching for affirmation and significance. Paul writes in 1 Corinthians 1:26-27, "For consider your calling, brothers: not many of you were wise according to worldly standards, not many were powerful, not many were of noble birth. But God chose what is foolish in the world to shame the wise; God chose what is weak in the world to shame the strong" (ESV).

What Paul describes above should resonate deeply with black lives. We, then, must embrace the realities of weakness and disenfranchisement, not as experiences worthy of shame, but the very ground that nurtures the seed of God's power and wisdom into a transforming force.

DIVERSITY IN THE GOSPELS

It is impossible to understand the biblical narrative without paying attention to the role that ethnic diversity plays. No one is truly colorblind. Claiming to be denies the beauty of a diverse humanity. It evades the value that color brings to the human experience. It preserves prejudice when we pretend not to see what is obviously there. And, it overlooks historical baggage that has shaped the social experience.

In the ancient world, ethnicity was a defining marker of social status. It was a social determinant for clean and unclean along with many other social stigmas. We see this clearly in one of the more popular parables of Jesus known as the parable of the Good Samaritan in Luke 10:25-37.

The phrase *good Samaritan* has become synonymous with a person who is kind and generous to the needy. However, the audience listening to Jesus' parable at the time despised the Samaritans as an ethnic group. Jesus tells this parable in response to a lawyer who posed the question, "Who is my neighbor?" With the parable, Jesus uses a Samaritan man—a person regarded as an outcast, untrustworthy, and ethnically impure—to teach a lesson about neighborliness. In doing so, he highlights not only what hospitality should look like, but also how God identifies with society's rejects.

Another example that displays ethnicity as a social status is the story of Jesus' encounter with the woman at the well in John 4. When she approaches, Jesus asks her for a drink of water, to which she responds, "How is it that you, a Jew, ask for a drink from me, a woman of Samaria?" (John 4:9 ESV). Jesus pays no heed to the ethnic segregation of his day because a central part of his mission was to embrace the outcast and the oppressed. To the Samaritan woman's surprise, Jesus demonstrates God's intolerance of both historic factions between people groups and gender oppression. Long before civil rights protesters sought to drink from "whites only" fountains, Jesus led by reaching across the segregated lines to request a drink from a Samaritan woman. Jesus is our model of resistance to all forms of bigotry and racial hierarchy. Black spirituality must pattern itself after the example of our Lord and Savior.

SEEING TRUE REPENTANCE IN THE GOSPELS

I once heard a preacher in a mostly white congregation say, "We're all equal at the foot of Jesus, there is no black or white, rich or poor, Jesus embraces all." Such sentiments are often met by loud, re-sounding "Amens," as many are glad to be received by God just as they are—no ifs or buts. And this is true. Jesus is no respecter of persons. We all enter into God's kingdom through the same pathway of repentance, receiving freedom from the power of sin and submitting to Christ's rule over our lives.

> Repentance is not merely abstract or metaphysical. It manifests itself in the particulars of our lives.

However, this is the view from several thousand feet in the air. On the ground, the application of these same steps looks unique for each person and context because the manifestations of sin in our lives and societies don't all look the same. Repenting of personal sins looks different from person to person. While rebuking complacent crowds, John the Baptist demands that they "bear fruits in keeping with repentance." To this, the crowd responds, "What then shall we do?" What John says next is, I believe, a shock to the system of Western Christianity: "Whoever has two tunics is to share with him who has none, and whoever has food is to do likewise." To the tax collectors who were often corrupt, he said, "Collect no more than you are authorized to do." To the soldiers who inquired what repentance looked like for them, he said, "Do not extort money from anyone by threats or by false accusation" (Luke 3:7-14 ESV). Repentance is not merely abstract or metaphysical. It manifests itself in the particulars of our lives. It looks to address and correct previous wrongdoing, particularly in the ways we have refused to care for others out of our abundance and in the many ways we have used our power to oppress the vulnerable. For Christians in the American context, this has huge implications for race relations. A colorblind ideology committed to ignoring the injustices and inequities created by race is an attempt to avoid the cost of repentance. Is there any wonder why we fail to bear the right fruit? Reading the New Testament rightly leads us to recognize that redemption in Christ is not a historical amnesia. Our ethnic, cultural, and racial identities do not get erased.

THE SUFFERING OF JESUS

The cross is a global symbol of the Christian faith. In ancient Rome, the cross was the means for carrying out the death penalty. The Roman Empire used this brutal tactic to enforce its authority and silence opposition. By executing criminals in a public crucifixion and leaving their dead bodies hanging up for days, their death became spectacle to antagonize the community and elicit fear. This was how Jesus died.

In post-slavery America, more than four thousand lynchings of African Americans occurred between 1877 and 1950. Throughout the South, racial terror chased after blacks who attempted to subvert the oppressive Jim Crow laws or pursue lives of dignity and freedom. After Reconstruction efforts were successfully hindered, white-black relationships took a violently antagonistic turn. Black bodies were no longer prized possessions in need of protection; they had become an economic commodity. As a result, they were seen as inconvenient at best and disposable at worst. This led to a wave of lynchings, racial terror, and riots. Black men, women, and children were brutally apprehended, beaten, and strung up in front of teeming mobs watching with murderous fervor.

The collective history of black America bears cultural memory of the trauma. In *The Cross and the Lynching Tree*, the late theologian James H. Cone points out that a significant part of the black Christian tradition is the embodiment of common ground with a suffering Jesus. He, too, was offered up to be killed by a teeming mob and a complicit and corrupt government. For black folks, when we mourn and grieve the wickedness of human beings and unjust power, we don't grieve in isolation. Our Savior has gone this way before us. He grieved in the very same way about the very same experiences.

> The cross of Christ is not merely symbolic of abstract theologies and orthodox propositions. It is a divine expression of solidarity with suffering people and supernatural victory that brings hope in the middle of human suffering.

We find in Jesus an empathetic and compassionate Savior. We don't have to explain our pain and sorrow. We don't need to justify the reality of our generational trauma. He knows intuitively because he also experienced the full depravity of sin expressed through a violent mob demanding death.

The cross of Christ is not merely symbolic of abstract theologies and orthodox propositions. It is a divine expression of solidarity with suffering people and supernatural victory that brings hope in the middle of human suffering. I once heard black theologian Willie Jennings capture this connection by saying, "Why did enslaved Africans become Christian? Despised flesh was drawn to the despised flesh of Christ."

A Christianity that meddles in "cheap grace" and is full of clichés is off-putting for people who suffer under the duress of structural evil. Dietrich Bonhoeffer says, "Cheap grace is the preaching of forgiveness without requiring repentance, baptism without church discipline, Communion without confession, absolution without personal confession. Cheap grace is grace without discipleship, grace without the cross, grace without Jesus Christ, living and incarnate." A Christianity that fails to boldly engage the experience of suffering people falls in the category of "cheap grace." It overlooks human pain in pursuit of a savior who is able to heal pain. The Holy Spirit empowers believers to be Christ's presence in a suffering world. Stated another way, Christians are Jesus' concrete presence that transcends place and time to advance God's mission of love.

Moreover, Christians must lament over injustice and suffering. Psalm 34:18 (ESV) says, "The LORD is near to the brokenhearted and saves the crushed in spirit." The nearness of God to those crushed in spirit is most evident in our Lord Jesus Christ himself. The author of Hebrews reminds us of this when he writes, "Since then we have a great high priest who has passed through the heavens, Jesus the son of God, let us hold fast our confession. For we do not have a high priest unable to sympathize with our weaknesses, but one who in every respect has been tempted as we are, yet without sin" (Hebrews 4:14-15 ESV).

Hebrews presents our Lord as one who bears with us in our suffering because he chose to join us in it. This Jesus is the one from whom black spirituality can draw deep meaning in order to find sustaining hope.

LIVING IT OUT

Reading the Bible through the colors of culture changes the way diverse people understand God, the world, and themselves. The Bible and the Christian message have journeyed a long way to meet us in twenty-first century America. Along the way, they have been redefined and repurposed by a wide range of doctrines and interpretations. Many of these have been helpful, but some have been outright destructive.

One of these destructive outcomes is that the good news of Jesus no longer sounds like good news to the very people near to his heart. However, because the world has no lack of people yearning for liberation, there are always people whose social reality should provoke with us a desire to revisit the Scriptures. Through their eyes, it is possible to correct our way of thinking. This means, however, that we must take the lives and experiences of the "least of these" as seriously as Jesus did. Jesus was always concerned about the sick, overlooked, marginalized, and socially oppressed people.

In America, the "least of these" category lands squarely on its oppressed minorities. Hence, the black perspective is pivotal for the development of a healthy Christian spirituality that practices the way of Christ. The stones that the builder rejected must become the cornerstone.

CHAPTER NINE

SOCIAL JUSTICE AND THE BIBLE

If we love God, we love what God loves; we develop a passion for
what God is passionate about. God is passionate about justice. God
is no respecter of persons. (Deuteronomy 10:17; Acts 10:34-35)

Mitzi J. Smith

Today, a culturally diverse army of white, black, Latino, Native
American, Asian, and other urban young people champion
social justice because it is a common moral good. They tend to
separate morality from faith claims, but the original concept of
social justice was a moral claim founded on Christian principles.
Social justice is, therefore, a practical point of connection between
the church and this generation. Unfortunately, many conservative
Christians demur the phrase "social justice" in favor of new language, such as "biblical justice" or "kingdom justice." They typically
limit their justice concerns to a few right-winged political interests
such as abortion, human trafficking, and a watered-down claim on
the pursuit of racial reconciliation.

For instance, a group of evangelical pastors and leaders drafted
"The Statement on Social Justice and the Gospel," which paints a
broad stroke over the issue of social justice. They argue that social
justice has taken on a so-called liberal agenda. So to distance themselves from the politically liberal, they abandon the language of

"social justice" for fear of being misconstrued with the so-called liberal camp. However, many conservative evangelicals tend to lose sight of the seriousness of a society plagued by the sin of social injustice. Sadly, they say they preach against sin but do very little to challenge sinful systems that colonized forms of Christianity set in motion—systems that have perpetuated social injustice. "The Statement on Social Justice and the Gospel" disregards the origin of the language of social justice.

Historically, social justice started as a Christian afront to social elitism and ethnic oppression. As Michael D. Palmer and I explain in our series *The Holy Spirit and Social Justice*, "The Italian Roman Catholic Jesuit scholar, Luigi Taparelli D'Azeglio (1793–1862), is generally credited with being the first to use the expression *social justice*." The language of social justice communicates the idea of making right a social problem with the authority of Christian sources. Rephrasing the language to "biblical" or "kingdom justice" is problematic because it designates the Bible or the kingdom as the point of concern. Social justice demands a focus on society's problems, a necessary concern that conservative Christians have disregarded for centuries. As Spirit-filled, Bible-believing theologian Kenneth Archer puts it, "Social justice is the Spirit's cry for the poor and the marginalized, for creation polluted and in decay, and for the victimizers and victims. Healing is found in relationship with Christ and his communities and in just societies."

> The Gospels reveal that salvation is about not only reconciling fallen humanity to God, but also caring about others in the throes of life.

Throughout the Gospels, Jesus demonstrates love, showing his followers that true love is attending to the needs of others. For instance, Matthew describes Jesus inviting those who are burdened with the hustle and bustle of life to rest in him (Matthew 11:28). Luke depicts Jesus with the sole mission of opening blinded eyes, liberating captives, and lifting oppression (Luke 4:18-19). In John, Jesus includes women and overcomes generations of ethnic factions to show that God seeks out who will simply accept his acceptance (John 4). The Gospels reveal that salvation is about not only reconciling fallen humanity to God, but also caring about others in the throes of life.

PROPHETIC COMPASSION

The truest form of social justice considers the situations of the world with deep, prayerful, and action-oriented compassion. Before picking up the Bible to start quoting passages that condemn the world, we must remember that Jesus did not come to condemn the world. He came so that the world might be delivered through him (John 3:17). In other words, the only perfect one came without eyes of condemnation, but with a heart of compassion. His compassion was not our usual pity on those not up to par. Rather, the compassion of Christ was a fiercely prophetic one. It was akin to what Old Testament scholar Walter Brueggemann calls "prophetic imagination and ministry." Prophetic imagination is task-oriented. Brueggemann explains, "The task of prophetic imagination and ministry is *to bring to public expression those very hopes and yearnings* that have been denied so long and suppressed so deeply that we no longer know they are there."

We must, as Karl Barth puts it, "hold the Bible in one hand and the newspaper in the other." Once we do this, we will see how the Bible informs social commentary of the times and how it can offer a valuable perspective in the public square. We could thus think of the Bible as a diagnostic manual of sorts—a tool we use to correctly identify the real issues and solutions.

In our nation's modern history, there's little understating of the role the Bible played during the civil rights movement. Opponents of the movement showcased an ugly side of America entrenched in a political and racial ideology that saw blacks as second-class citizens at best and subhuman animals at worst. While the Bible is not designed to be a political document like, say, the US Constitution, it paints a very clear picture of God as the supreme authority from which all other authority on earth is derived. Having this top-down view of politics allows Christians to critique the injustices committed by earthly governments, as well as morally justify the activism that seeks to correct those injustices.

The Bible-based mechanism that strengthens Christian activism is called repentance. Many of the external struggles we face—personally and socially—stem from internal struggles. By repenting of our personal and social sins, we're able to take responsibility for those struggles and work toward resolving them. It was not a series of courtroom victories that led to the major successes of the civil rights movement, but a series of spiritual victories in the hearts and minds of Americans everywhere. Our nation could not have gotten there without the work of Martin Luther King Jr. and other Christian leaders who called for change. It took black and white Christians to make a difference. And it will take all of us to embrace a unifying vision of Christianity to take back contemporary minds from the brinks of skepticism.

King's biblical understanding of social justice allowed the civil rights movement to focus on the soul of America itself and whether it could be saved from the sins of slavery and white supremacy. For better or for worse, our Founding Fathers took the *wait and see* approach when it came to abolition and universal suffrage, but they at least provided the foundation for these movements in the preamble to the Declaration of Independence.

DREAMING OF JUSTICE

In 1963, King delivered his famous "I Have a Dream" speech and referenced the Declaration's preamble as a "promissory note," one that America had defaulted on. The speech became a clarion call in the civil rights movement and also for the casual American bystander. It was an admonishment for the nation to drop the *wait and see* approach and take a *look and act* approach instead. King's point reached its crescendo in the speech when he painted a picture of what it would take to satisfy the civil rights movement:

And as we walk, we must make the pledge that we shall always march ahead. We cannot turn back.

There are those who are asking the devotees of civil rights, "When will you be satisfied?" We can never be satisfied as long as the Negro is the victim of the unspeakable horrors of police brutality. We can never be satisfied as long as our bodies, heavy with the fatigue of travel, cannot gain lodging in the motels of the highways and the hotels of the cities. We cannot be satisfied as long as the Negro's basic mobility is from a smaller ghetto to a larger one. We can never be satisfied as long as our children are stripped of their selfhood and robbed of their dignity by signs stating "For Whites Only." We cannot be satisfied as long as a Negro in Mississippi cannot vote and a Negro in New York believes he has nothing for which to vote. No, no, we are not satisfied and we will not be satisfied until justice rolls down like waters and righteousness like a mighty stream.

Throughout King's speech, his associates could be heard in the background affirming him, almost egging him on, in a sense to put the script down and start preaching! Eventually, King went totally off script and began his "I have a Dream" refrain. At that point, King started preaching. The language King used in the above quote was inspired by a biblical view of justice, which echoed the writing of the prophet Amos: "Though you offer Me burnt offerings and your grain offerings, I will not accept *them*, Nor will I regard your fattened peace offerings. Take away from Me the noise of your songs, For I will not hear the melody of your stringed instruments. But let justice run down like water, And righteousness like a mighty stream" (Amos 5:22-24 NKJV).

The kind of justice Amos refers to in the text is not a legalistic kind, but a holistic one. The prophet is saying that God does not want superficial forms of devotion or sacrifice, but for us to show our true obedience by doing justice. The contrast here is similar to the points King drew on in his speech. For instance, simply removing "For Whites Only" signs would not be enough to satisfy the dream. The signs were offensive, but they didn't encompass the suffering that people of color endured at the time. King understood the biblical message to be a prophetic call for the fullness of justice. He drew from the wells of Christian resources to rediscover that in Jesus real equality is achievable. This is why King's speeches and his usage of biblical words and phrases were so powerful.

King, furthermore, exposed the hypocrisy among Christians of his day. They claimed a faith of love but did not extend love to help suffering people. On a broader societal level, the fire of repentance King stoked against racism was the same fire the English Abolitionists had stirred up two centuries prior, a fire started by Christians who saw slavery as an evil to be purged from their land. William Wilberforce, a champion of the Abolition movement, wrote of faith in action in 1823:

> While efforts are making to rescue our country from this guilt and this reproach, let everyone remember that he is answerable for any measure of assistance which Providence has enabled him to render towards the accomplishment of the good work. In a country in which the popular voice has a powerful and constitutional influence on the government and legislation, to be silent when there is a question of reforming abuses repugnant to justice and humanity is to share their guilt. Power always implies responsibility; and the possessor of it cannot innocently be neutral, when by his exertion moral good may be promoted, or evil lessened or removed.

Wilberforce's fervor to dismantle not only the slave trade but also chattel slavery itself was motivated by a genuine desire to do justice and love mercy. The role of personal responsibility was a consistent theme in Wilberforce's writings when it came to social justice. Because slavery was a sin against your fellow man, he viewed it as a sin against God as well. Getting right with God, then, requires making things right with our fellow man. I would hesitate to call this a works-based theology because what Wilberforce was truly going after was works consistent with theology. Any Christian who, therefore, does not put their faith into action is not living as Christ himself acted.

King was no stranger to highlighting the need for personal responsibility either. For instance, in a sermon he gave in 1957 titled "Conquering Self-Centeredness," King points out that one's self-centeredness drives egotistical and irresponsible behaviors. If one lets self-centeredness go unchecked, it will eventually result in madness. King's prescription for this problem was to embrace others-centeredness. He saw Wilberforce as an example of how to do just that. King says,

> And the way to solve this problem is not to drown out the ego but to find your sense of importance in something outside of the self. And you are then able to live because you have given your life to something outside and something that is meaningful, objectified. You rise above this self-absorption to something outside. We look through history. We see that biography is a running commentary of this. We see a Wilberforce. We see him somehow satisfying his desire by absorbing his life in the slave trade, those who are victims of the slave trade. We see a Florence Nightingale. We see her finding meaning and finding a sense of belonging by giving herself to a great cause, to the unnursed wounded. We see an Albert Schweitzer who looks at men in dark Africa who have been the victims of colonialism and imperialism and there he gives his life to that. He objectifies himself in this great cause. And then we can even find Jesus totally objectifying himself when

he cries out, "Ye have done it unto the least of these my brethren, ye have done it unto me."

Self-centeredness can be personal or tribal. Personal self-centeredness focuses on an individual. Tribal self-centeredness lifts an ethnicity, or so-called race, or nationality as superior with special standing in the world and in the sight of God.

WHAT CAN WE LEARN FROM SCRIPTURE?

Christianity is all about social justice. A people once alienated from God are now called to return to him and rediscover their godlikeness through Jesus Christ. A careful read of Scripture and a grasp of historical context reveal how far off base elitist interpretations of the Bible and expressions of Christianity really are. The Bible empowers the powerless and liberates the oppressed through the personal and social saving grace of Jesus. Bible believers are able to become woke by seeing other people the way God sees them—made in his image. Traditionally, this concept is known as the *imago Dei*, or "image of God," which is grounded in Genesis 1:27. It means that all human beings are equal. God has imparted a divine spark within humanity. Within this concept we find the strength to repent from both self-centeredness and race-centeredness. We can understand racism by thinking of it in terms of rejecting the image of God in others.

The Ten Commandments are all expressions of different ways we should respect the image of God. Each one focuses on how we're supposed to honor God and honor others. When we do that, we'll stop killing each other in the name of God. We'll stop stealing, cheating, and coveting the things our neighbor owns. We'll become God-centered without losing our personal identity.

One useful illustration is that of a rainbow. If we think of God as the pure light, then humanity is the colorful rainbow produced by that light. Every human being is a being of color, each with unique energy and passion that we use to color the world. God has a plan to use each of us, like a painter who mixes a full palette of colors to complete his masterpiece. Who are we, then, to tell the painter which colors are useless? What gives any of us the right to turn to another human being and deny their contribution to the world simply by living in it?

On the other hand, it is equally as problematic to move in the opposite direction and neutralize all sense of identity whatsoever. One classic popular passage used in this regard comes from Colossians, which reads: "Do not lie to each other, since you have taken off your old self with its practices and have put on the new self, which is being renewed in knowledge in the image of its Creator. Here there is no Gentile or Jew, circumcised or uncircumcised, barbarian, Scythian, slave or free, but Christ is all, and is in all" (Colossians 3:9-11).

At first glance, this passage seems to radically neutralize one's personal identity, but it's really grounding our identity first in the image of God and second in Christ himself. The new self that we put on is empowered by the knowledge of the image of God, which always clothes us in our personal contexts, regardless of our skin color, country of origin, or religious preference. What the new self tells us is that we are no longer beholden to our personal context in terms of our relationship with God. It simply does not matter what your gender, ethnicity, sexuality, or politics are when it comes to worshiping God because he is beyond all of those things. No matter who you are or where you live, you can come to Christ.

One aspect of our identity that I see the church struggling with is affirming our dual citizenship as both citizens in the kingdom of heaven and citizens in the nations and tribes of this world. I'm reminded of one of the most important lessons I learned and later taught in seminary: It's both/and. It's always tempting to bifurcate issues and think of them in binary either/or terms, but in the case of our dual citizenship it's both/and. We are *both* citizens of the kingdom of heaven *and* citizens in the nations and tribes of this world. The image presented by the book of Revelation reminds us powerfully of this fact: "After this I looked, and there before me was a great multitude that no one could count, from every nation, tribe, people and language, standing before the throne and before the Lamb. They were wearing white robes and were holding palm branches in their hands" (Revelation 7:9).

Notice here that the multitude is *both* from every nation *and* standing before the throne. This affirmation of worldly identity assures us that we can all come together and be the church despite our differences. The church, as God intends, consists of people of all nations, cultures, and languages. It is not—nor does it belong to—any one nation, culture, and language. In the church, we have the opportunity to experience that completeness of color, a united front with anyone and everyone facing the throne of God. How can we face the throne of God when we have not learned that God is a God of diversity?

TOWARD A THEOLOGY OF IDENTITY AND SOCIAL JUSTICE

So what does all of this talk of identity have to do with social justice? Once we sort out our identity, we won't face confusion about *whose* justice we're pursuing. Once we acknowledge that we're all children of God made in his image, we will come to see that an injustice upon one of us is an injustice upon all of us. That's what social justice really means. Without taking into consideration a biblical view of identity, social justice projects will become corrupted by the agendas and politics of the world. If our identity is based entirely on a single tribe or ideology rather than a biblical one, our view of justice will follow suit. For example, we are quick to judge a referee's call when it goes against the team we're supporting, but when it's against the other team it's no big deal.

The answer isn't to disregard our contextual gifts from birth, such as ethnic and cultural identities, but rather to acknowledge it wholeheartedly, and surrender it as a gift among many. Show Southern pride. Root for the Cowboys or Patriots (okay I will stop while I am ahead!). Tell everybody that your city is the greatest city in the world. Yet, our full identity is in community with all of God's people. Together, we are God's image!

LIVING IT OUT

Scripture values engaging the situations of the world with prophetic compassion. Life helps us interpret Scripture and Scripture guides the faithful to the liberating love of God in Christ. Examples such as Wilberforce and King pondered the revelation of God's love for everyone in the face of insurmountable hate and abuse directed at God's people. They were convicted that professing Christians who participated in the slave trade and Jim Crow laws used God as a cover for their own greed and pride. Holding the situations of the world in one hand and the Bible in the other, Wilberforce, King, and others contradicted religious hate with God's love and counterattacked abuse with godly defiance that led revolutions of social justice.

We do not need a new name for social justice. We need to employ biblical faith that attends to the cries of those who suffer social injustice. When properly understood, Christianity empowers the powerless and liberates the oppressed. This must be the Christian mission because it was the mission of the founder of the faith. Scripture teaches not only about a Christ who offers personal salvation, but one who also brings hope for social salvation, which is the heart of social justice.

PART FOUR

WHERE DO
WE GO FROM HERE?
THE STREETS ARE
WAITING

CHAPTER TEN

A NEW WAY TO THINK
ABOUT THE FAITH

Whoever loves has been born of God and knows God.

1 JOHN 4:7

I t is important that although most of the people throughout the Bible were people of color, the tenor of Scripture points beyond ethnicity to a God who invites everyone to live as sisters and brothers. The Holy Spirit then empowers the church to extend this invitation to all of the world. We must listen to the Spirit and obey the Spirit's leading.

Church is where believers prepare to go into the neighborhoods to share the good news of Jesus Christ. We must listen to the cries that are there. By listening, we not only discover needs but also discover God's presence that is already in the complexities of ordinary life.

When I first became a student prison chaplain, I thought I was going to take the Lord to the prisons. To my surprise, when I arrived, I found God was already there. I often tell people that I learned so much about God through spiritual encounters in the prison. Like the woman who met Jesus at the well in John 4, I told everyone I knew that God is in the prisons. My life changed and so did my theology.

As a musician, I knew how to find God in beautiful pictures and sounds. But now I discovered a deeper revelation. I found God in brokenness, and it changed my ministry forever. Over the past twenty years, my own life challenges have strengthened my conviction. I can testify that God is closest to us in the vicissitudes of life. No wonder I found God in the prisons! But so many people who are going through hard times cannot see God.

> The colorful Bible bears witness that no particular gender, nationality, or culture has a monopoly on the faith of Jesus. Biblical Christianity is God's love expressed in Jesus Christ. Jesus came to redeem a fractured world to the likeness of God.

The Christian task is first to be fully present with people. Then, with an approach of humility, express love, grace, and hope. The Holy Spirit opens their eyes as the Spirit also opens ours. So many people need to know that God is on the side of the wounded. It is our duty to show them!

Given the upsurge of suspicion about faith, the Christian mission must not focus on growing churches. It must turn its gaze toward showing the world how Jesus came to love them, affirm their humanity, and offer them hope in despair.

LISTEN, WATCH, LEARN, AND PARTICIPATE

To give a straight answer to the title question of this book, Christianity is a faith that affirms all of humanity equally in God's eyes. Both women and men in the ethnic and cultural kaleidoscope of human diversity are a reflection of God's beauty. The colorful Bible bears witness that no particular gender, nationality, or culture has a monopoly on the faith of Jesus. Biblical Christianity is God's love expressed in Jesus Christ. Jesus came to redeem a fractured world to the likeness of God. Any historical or current monopoly on the faith insults the purpose of the incarnation.

Jesus came to offer hope to everyone. What impressed Luke, who was a Roman physician and the writer of the two biblical volumes of the Gospel of Luke and Acts, was that God sent Jesus to extend his love to all the nations of the world. Luke's two volumes are filled with examples of how Jesus includes the excluded. So how in the world did Christian history evolve into so much bigotry, elitism, and hatefulness?

God made his love for all of humanity very clear to the very prejudiced disciple named Peter. As a first-century Palestinian Jew, all of Peter's life he was taught that those who were not Jewish were unclean. Peter carried his cultural biases into the ministry. God dealt with his life-long cultural stereotypes through an encounter with a household of Italians in Acts 10. God showed Peter his love for the very people Peter did not care for. God sent people to Cornelius and his household to share the gospel. And that whole European family converted to Christianity. When Peter saw Cornelius and his household come to faith, he had a moment of revelation and exclaimed, "I now realize how true it is that God does not show favoritism but accepts from every nation the one who fears him and does what is right" (Acts 10:34-35).

None of Jesus' parables, sermons, and teachings belong to one nation, tribe, or ethnic group. The faith that originated with Jews quickly expanded when missionaries carried the gospel to other people and nations. The early Christian message was that faith offers participation in God's family. Regardless of one's racial or ethnic origin, regardless of one's life story, they belong in God's family.

Any racial, ethnic, or even denominational monopoly on the faith undermines God's vision. So God needed to purify Peter's vision of the faith. Otherwise, the disciple who Jesus charged to feed the flock of God (John 21:17) would have missed out on his own calling. Likewise, contemporary Christians miss the mark when they explicitly, complicity, or in any way take part in racism, xenophobia, anti-Semitism, Islamophobia, misogyny, and any other bigotry. These are demonic tools used to sabotage the Christian mission to unify the global image of God.

WHERE'S THE CHRISTIAN PARTY?

This generation is in urgent need of a new vision for racial and ethnic diversity. The world is becoming more integrated. The United States is more diverse than ever. The history of racism is now colliding with the future of an America that is more colorful than ever. Faith-led racial conciliation is necessary. Without it, a diverse nation risks tribal factions that will inevitably lead to unnecessary battles and possibly even civil war.

Young people are yearning for a spirituality that affirms social justice in a world of social pain. Justice and righteousness are the hallmark of Jesus' message, but public religious statements on social issues often seem more concerned about what is believed than the hurting people who are alienated by such statements. It is imperative that Christians refrain from judging the LGBTQ community, victims of rape and abuse, formerly incarcerated persons, the homeless, drug addicts, and people from other religious traditions. There are no special sets of sinners just as there are no special groups of Christians. God's love will do whatever internal work that needs to be done.

Imagine that instead of instructing Peter to "feed my sheep," Jesus had said, "Be sure you announce your doctrine and political affiliation." The idea may seem laughable, but mainstream and evangelical churches in America may be doing just that—twisting the gospel into a confessional religion and a political platform.

A few years ago, there was a political debate in Virginia Beach. I was not sure if I wanted to go, so I did not end up getting a ticket. By chance, I saw a guy I knew who was going to the debate. He had an extra ticket and randomly asked me if I was going. I told him I really wanted to go but didn't have a ticket. He responded with a question: "Are you pro-life? Because I have a ticket for anyone who is pro-life." What he was really saying was, "I will give you a ticket if you are Republican."

To be honest, I was taken aback because the well-meaning young man was more concerned that I share his politics than that I share his faith. He already knew I am a dedicated Christian, but he needed to be sure that I was the kind of Christian that agrees with his politics. Otherwise, he was willing to keep a second ticket that he could not use.

I try to be pro-all-of-life (womb to tomb). I think that is what Jesus wants. But I am not sure if there is a political party that would align with my commitment to follow Jesus. The church is Jesus' political entity. Party politics can never take the place of the church, and the struggle within the American church to assign God's will to a particular political party is a misrepresentation of Jesus Christ.

There must remain tension between church and state—remaining in conversation but keeping a wall between the two is good. However, there are forces at work that either try to remove that wall or to build the wall higher. The squabbles about party politics among Christians are not helpful to win young people back to the faith. The Jesus that millennials are most likely to be attracted to is the one who invites sinners over for dinner. He is the one most focused on the hurts and needs in the community. He is the one who glorifies God over presidents and kings.

> **The church is Jesus' political entity. Party politics can never take the place of the church.**

Christians have two options: we can retreat from the public square altogether, or double down and bear witness to the re-visioning of faith that affirms all people. There is a time and place for retreating, but Christians must no longer acquiesce.

What, then, can the local church do to get uninterested young people back?

WORK TOWARD ATTRACTING YOUNG PEOPLE

In and out of the classroom, I've worked with non-traditional students, college students, and teens. One thing is for sure—people are people. Everyone wants to be loved, affirmed, and included. I wish there were a silver bullet solution to repopulate our churches with millennials. I am often asked for my advice on how to engage this generation, and I've found that whether they are a pastor or business owner, the same points apply equally to both.

Since young people are growing up faster than they used to, and parents are not as present in their lives, an important step to getting them engaged is consensus building. They want their voices heard. They want to feel like they are part of the solution. The Holy Spirit's presence within the church empowers believers to listen and interpret what other people need. The miracle of Pentecost in Acts 2 is more about hearing and understanding the language of another than speaking in another language.

Next, we must recognize that times have changed. God's unchangeability is adjustable to changing times. This means that while the nature of God does not change, God's method is adjustable to where people are. Young people connect to the world with their phones and laptops, so you have to give them something to connect to that looks current. Today's generation experiences life digitally.

Additionally, Christians must be authentic. Keep it real! While no one is perfect but God, God calls believers to faithfulness. Realness is not perfection—realness is faithfulness. Millennials relate to authority differently than the previous generation. They do not have to listen and follow. The "telling them what to do" approach fails miserably. They are more apt to follow that which they perceive to be real. Now is the time to refrain from hyperspiritual claims about being "blessed and highly favored."

We must admit that sometimes living seems to take the life out of us—even believers. It is the grace of God that loves us in our wounded and helpless state. Our sincerity and faithfulness to a

God who is on the side of the broken compels people to the faith. It also draws other broken people in search of solutions to ask about our faith. Keeping it real gives Christians street cred that brings the right to be heard. In other words, authenticity earns the authority we need to share our faith.

PARACHURCH GROUPS AS ARMS OF THE CHURCH

Some of my colleagues believe there's no such thing as "parachurch organizations" (PCOs) because we're all one as the body of Christ. Others argue that PCOs should serve as extensions of a local church. I argue that all ministries must serve as extensions of the local church. This includes Christian colleges and universities, seminaries and schools of theology. In 1 Corinthians 12:27, Paul calls the church the body of Christ. All PCOs, including those that engage in the practice of ministry and those that train ministers, are most effective when they attend to God's mission in and through the church.

There are many existing PCOs that respond to particular needs in society, including InterVarsity Christian Fellowship, Operation Blessing, Fellowship of Christian Athletes, Chi Alpha, Cru (Campus Crusade for Christ), Alpha, Youth With A Mission, Young Life, Kanye West's Sunday Service, Gideons International, the Urban Renewal Center, Jakes Divinity School, Texas Offenders Re-entry Initiative, and United Mega Care. These organizations have resources tailored to their contexts. Many of them have clear and intentional connections with local churches. The Urban Renewal Center is in partnership with the First Presbyterian Church of Norfolk and other local churches in Norfolk, Virginia. Jakes Divinity School, Texas Offenders Re-entry Initiative, and United Mega Care are all PCOs that are in partnership with The Potter's House of Dallas.

In Matthew 16:18, Jesus says, "On this rock I will build my church." The church is God's idea, so any extensions must remain participants in Christ's mission for the church. Too often people with great zeal for God build PCOs because they have a passion for a particular ministry and are frustrated that their local church is not attending to the need as effectively as they think they should. However, every believer is called to be part of the body of Christ. To ensure that new believers are properly involved in a local body of believers, parachurch ministries need a seamless connection with the local church. Otherwise, their efforts are relegated to humanitarian efforts, or worse, they share God's love in the world but perpetuate the epidemic of unchurched people.

When PCOs maintain commitment to a local body, they exemplify faithfulness to the work of Christ to make disciples of all ethnic (and/or racial) groups (Matthew 28:19). We must remember two things about the Great Commission. First, a divine command to go into the world requires the Spirit's guidance. Evangelism and outreach play an important role, yet Jesus gave his followers the Great Commission to go into the world to make disciples.

Second, the commission to make disciples is daunting without a pattern to follow. Jesus discipled his followers because to make disciples one must also be discipled. As Jesus did it, so must his followers. Discipleship involves teaching and spiritual formation that happens in the context of a local fellowship. Discipleship must, therefore, be the goal of every local church. People need a place of belonging to be formed into the likeness of Christ.

RE-ENVISIONING CHRISTIANITY FOR THE FUTURE

Western Christianity is in a state of emergency. With the decline in church attendance and the increase of "nones" (people who have no faith affiliation), every Christian must be concerned with the state of the faith. We need more creative avenues to extend the Christian reach. More importantly, it is imperative that pastors and Christian leaders seek a deeper understanding of the faith. In a spiritual desert, young people are growing unattracted to the church.

While it may be true that this generation is less interested in organized religion, it remains hungry for relationship with God. Young people continue to look for identity, love, hope, and spiritual solutions to everyday problems. PCOs are avenues for the church to move beyond the boxed-in experience of faith and be creative. Also, PCOs are great ministry resources to partner with other community organizations. Creative partnerships may be on-ramps for people who are reluctant to attend church but curious about what faith has to offer.

The church must also take seriously this generation's hunger for spiritual discovery. At its inception, the church of Jesus Christ placed a premium on the Holy Spirit's person, life, and mission. The Holy Spirit is God's presence in the hearts of believers to actualize God's work in the world, and local churches and PCOs are vehicles for the work of the Holy Spirit.

> **Local churches and PCOs are vehicles for the work of the Holy Spirit.**

Because people are not going to church like they used to, and the needs in the community are outgrowing the resources to address them, it seems that ministry has in many ways escaped traditional church practices. Many people are not likely to come to church, not even on Christmas, Easter, Mother's Day, or for a New Year's service. So, while *going out* is theologically sound, *going out* may be the only way to know who is in the world. There is a dire need for more ministry efforts in the communities. There is a great need for Christians to invest time and money in PCOs that extend the mission of the church in a hurting world.

Over the last few years, I sensed the Holy Spirit was calling me to attend to bridging the church with the community. This calling became clearer as the Black Lives Matter movement took over the news cycle. The reactions to these events was hopeful on some levels, but unsettling on others. I found it hopeful because Black

Lives Matter brought the conversation of racial reconciliation to the forefront. But with it came the unsettling reality of finally taking an introspective look at our own brokenness as a society. Our pride and prejudice finally began to reach a boiling point.

I left my full-time faculty position at Regent University and began laying the groundwork for the Urban Renewal Center (URC) in Norfolk. The mission of the URC is to awaken society to its promised wholeness. The URC is a conceptual center of Christian thought and action. Because it is a PCO, we've built partnerships with other churches and organizations in ways that some local churches can't. However, the work remains intimately connected with the mission of the local church.

I then moved to Dallas, Texas, to launch the Jakes Divinity School at The Potter's House. Bishop Jakes is an exemplary global leader with a desire to extend God's love beyond the walls of the church through faithful witness to Jesus Christ by the power of the Holy Spirit. The divinity school is an arm of the church to raise up leaders to carry the banner of faith forward. We must look beyond now to discern the times leading into the next century.

What should ministry look like for the twenty-second century?

Christian leaders must redeem the faith from perceptions that it's no more than a mechanism of power in the hands of good ol' boys. Ministry and ministry training must be vigilant to defend the faith in such a way that "extinguish[es] all the flaming arrows of the evil one" (Ephesians 6:16). The twenty-second century awaits ministries that are attuned to the technological revolution that has already begun. Ministries that are afraid of social media and resistant to incorporating contemporary technology will struggle to serve the needs in the world. Times are not regressing to rotary telephones and black and white televisions. It is imperative that we boldly bear witness in both the analog and digital spaces, and in all venues currently under development, such as artificial intelligence, quantum computing, and nanotechnology.

Theological education is an extension of the local church. It serves the need for ministerial formation for effective ministry in the church and society. For too long, seminaries have existed independent of the church. At best, they have looked to the church for students. But they have built their institutions as isolated ivy towers. However, the need for deeper study and more rigorous thinking demands scholars *of the church* to do research *for the church* and respond to tough questions including but not limited to race and racism, human sexuality, and systemic oppression.

For three years, Jesus taught his disciples to evangelize, disciple, teach, pastor, and, most importantly, what it means to love fellow human beings. There's a great need for theological schools that form innovative ministers to bear witness in a variety of areas such as business, neighborhoods, sports, cyberspace, and more. For this reason, at Jakes Divinity School we seek to nurture students to apply their hearts, heads, and hands—hearts of compassion and love for a fragile world in need of God's love, heads that wander in search of God's truth, and hands that work to advance the kingdom of God in the world.

Theological education must be positioned to harness the best of PCOs through innovative approaches for training ministers and pastors to impact the world. Importantly, theological education must also "keep it real!" People are no longer attending church simply because their families are Christians. However, people around the world are seeking spirituality that

> **The gospel is the good news that Jesus invites all of God's children to enjoy the abundance of life he has to offer.**

provides solutions to problems. Christians must be bold about their faith but share it with humility and compassion for a world that is increasingly faithless.

The world is waiting for *moral leadership* that defies the status quo and builds bridges between people. Everyone wants the same thing—to live well. The gospel is the good news that Jesus invites all of God's children to enjoy the abundance of life he has to offer. Jesus does not limit his promise of well-being to white, black, brown, or yellow people. His promise is suitable for everyone. Therefore, any monopoly on God's love, grace, and blessings is a diabolical stronghold in need of sharp objection.

I can't overemphasize the need for Christians to engage in *conversations about faith and culture*. Despite a difficult history, our faith remains vibrant and practical for today's world. Christianity does not belong to any particular people who use it for social supremacy or nationalist agendas. Biblical Christianity is about a God who loves the world—the *whole* world. It is about a God who redeems all of humanity through Jesus Christ.

RECENTERING GOD'S LOVE IN CHRISTIANITY

The characters in Scripture are indeed a reflection of God's colorful world. The integrity of faith that exudes from the Bible affirms every single human being as an equal reflection of God's image. John 3:16 says, "For God so loved the world that he gave his one and only Son, that whoever believes in him shall not perish but have eternal life." Christians quote this all the time. But have we learned the full meaning of a God who loves more than white people, more than black people, or more than Jews? God loves the world! This means that God loves everyone equally regardless of race, ethnicity, gender, religion, background, economic status, or ability. And so should we love each other.

I hope you rise to the occasion and show God's love like never before—a love that is better acted upon than said. Love addresses structural concerns with an eye on equal treatment of all people. We need the power and guidance of the Holy Spirit to re-engage the world, to apply our hearts, heads, and hands—hearts of compassion for a fragile society in need of God's love, heads that wonder in pursuit of the Spirit's guidance, and hands that work to advance the fullness of God's love in a world of many ethnicities, languages, and social locations.

It's past time to cease and desist, contest and resist the perpetuation of a faith that elevates privilege for some and oppresses others. Christianity emerged from a colorful Bible with human equality as its vision. What we have experienced is an abuse of Scripture and a travesty of the faith of Jesus. The resurgence of supremacy and elitism continues to peak its ugly head in a time of religious and political syncretism. As it has always been, the corruption of global Christianity has hinged on greed of money and power at the expense of the faith.

The faith of Jesus Christ does not sanction greed-sponsored elitism, bigotry, or hate, nor does it retaliate with elitism, bigotry, or hate. In the famous words of Dr. Martin Luther King Jr., "Returning hate for hate multiplies hate, adding deeper darkness to a night already devoid of stars. Darkness cannot drive out darkness; only light can do that. Hate cannot drive out hate; only love can do that."

Revisiting biblical history is necessary to rediscover God's love. A renewed vision of God's mission of love is refreshing. It reminds us that hate does not have the last word. And, it bolsters a positive vision that pierces through any grim circumstances. It

> **Jesus is God's expressed love for the entire world—even for those people who don't look like us.**

reminds us that Jesus came and experienced the horrors of earth's sorrows. But he showed us that the vicissitudes of life can only keep us down for so long. His resurrection gives us hope that whoever we are and wherever we are in life, we can rise again!

I pray that the pages of this book have helped to realign your spiritual awareness of both the world around us and the faith of Jesus. I hope that churches rethink their presence in their communities and seek ways to extend themselves beyond their walls. I hope that young people and emerging adults will experience a Christianity that has meaning and relevance for their everyday lives.

We all need to know that biblical history is full of contributions from the kaleidoscope of ethnic, cultural, and situational diversity. Followers of Jesus must live with an awareness that the image of God is reflected in every human being, and that Jesus is God's expressed love for the entire world—even for those people who don't look like us.

ACKNOWLEDGMENTS

The book is a product of many conversations. From the classroom to the church to the streets, there is much chatter about the state of Christianity. Its history is decorated with highs and lows, good and evil, ups and downs. At times, people in power have used the Bible and Christianity as a mechanism of oppression and even outright malevolence. As we look toward the middle of the twenty-first century, with all of society's complexities and social challenges, there is no doubt that once again the faith is on trial.

I owe a debt of gratitude to my agent Teresa Evenson at William K. Jensen Literary Agency for believing that this book is important "for such a time as this." I am grateful for my students who pushed me to rethink about the state and future of Christianity. I am thankful for those who read the manuscript at different stages, gave input on the various chapters, and provided moral support: Ross Wood, Pastor Jim Wood from the First Presbyterian Church of Norfolk, my family, and my colleagues at Jakes Divinity School in Dallas, Texas. I am particularly grateful for my team: Malaika Karriem, Alexander Fella, Joshua Lewis, Daniel Ortsejemine Amotsuka, and Gordon Tubbs. Without their assistance, the depth of thought presented here would not have been possible.

Lastly, and importantly, I wish to thank IVP for believing in this book and choosing to present it to the world. It has been such a pleasure working with the entire team from editing to graphics to marketing. I am delighted to be part of the IVP family!

NOTES

1. THE STRIKING QUESTION

9   *The slaves' historical identity*: Alvert J. Raboteau, *Slave Religion: The "Invisible Institution" in the Antebellum South* (New York: Oxford University Press, 2004), 251.

10 *A genuine leader*: Martin Luther King Jr. in Donald T. Phillips, *Martin Luther King, Jr. on Leadership* (New York: Hachette Book Group, 1998), 50.

13 *Black urban youth*: Dale P. Andrews, *Practical Theology for Black Churches: Bridging Black Theology & African American Folk Religion* (Louisville, KY: Westminster John Knox, 2002), 68.

14 *Pew Research reports*: "In U.S., Decline of Christianity Continues at Rapid Pace," Pew Research Center, October 17, 2019, www.pewforum.org/2019/10/17/in-u-s -decline-of-christianity-continues-at-rapid-pace.

2. A CRISIS OF FAITH

19 *Studies show that millennials*: Abigail Geiger, "Millennials Are the Most Likely Generation of Americans to Use Public Libraries," Pew Research Center, June 21, 2017, www.pewresearch.org/fact-tank/2017/06/21/millennials-are-the-most-likely -generation-of-americans-to-use-public-libraries.

    65% of American adults: "In U.S., Decline of Christianity Continues at Rapid Pace," Pew Research Center, October 17, 2019, www.pewforum.org/2019/10/17/in-u-s -decline-of-christianity-continues-at-rapid-pace.

20 *African Americans under the age of thirty*: Peter Beinart, "Breaking Faith," *Atlantic*, April 2017, www.theatlantic.com/magazine/archive/2017/04/breaking-faith /517785.

    When I tell people: Robert P. Jones and Daniel Cox, *Doing Church and Doing Justice: A Portrait of Millennials at Middle Church* (Washington, DC: Public Religion Institute, 2011), 6.

21 *millennials are hesitant*: Caroline Newman, "Why Millennials Are Leaving Religion but Embracing Spirituality," *UVA Today*, December 14, 2015, https://news.virginia .edu/content/qa-why-millennials-are-leaving-religion-embracing-spirituality.

22 *Only 32 percent . . . read the Bible*: Barna Group, "Millennials & the Bible 2014," 2014, www.americanbible.org/uploads/content/Millennials_and_the_Bible _Report_(Barna,_ABS__InterVarsity).pdf, 21.

    Twenty-none percent . . . are happy: Barna, "Millennials & the Bible 2014," 55.

    Only 10 percent . . . engage in Bible study: Barna, "Millennials & the Bible 2014," 33.

22   *15 percent . . . decreased Bible usage*: Barna, "Millennials & the Bible 2014," 30.

millennial skeptics: Barna, "Millennials & the Bible 2014," 51.

Steadily, it seems: Luna Malbroux, "Why More Young Black People Are Trading in Church for African Spirituality," Splinter, December 18, 2017, https://splinternews.com/why-more-young-black-people-are-trading-in-church-for-a-1821316608.

23   *DeShawn Tatem, also known as the Golden Child*: DeShawn Tatem, "Touched by an Angel at the ATM, CBN.com," The Christian Broadcasting Network, YouTube, April 22, 2008, https://youtu.be/Xs82WEm1S3o.

go where the church: DeShawn Tatem, "Gold Interview," Grown and Saved, YouTube, December 20, 2007, www.youtube.com/watch?v=QIVVNvSqV0c.

Tatem was once a member: "It's a Holy Hip-Hop Movement in Hampton Roads," *The Virginian-Pilot*, April 17, 2007, https://pilotonline.com/entertainment/article_8197fcba-2bfb-5bab-86a2-c053294f3af6.html.

Tatem's spiritual quest: "Obituary for General DeShawn Jermaine Tatem," Beach Funeral & Cremation Services, Inc., accessed March 4, 2018, www.beachfuneral andcremationservices.com/notices/GeneralDeShawn-Tatem.

24   *According to reports*: "Shooting Death Ruled Self-Defense by District Attorney," *Independent Tribune*, December 15, 2017, www.independenttribune.com/news /shooting-death-ruled-self-defense-by-district-attorney/article_448b244a-e1b5-11 e7-87ac-3bc4b02e9099.html.

the second option: Malbroux, "Why More Young Black People."

25   *that kind of Christian*: Stoyan Zaimov, "Carl Lentz Hesitates to Call Himself Evangelical, Says Term Has Been 'Hijacked,'" *Christian Post*, June 27, 2018, www .christianpost.com/news/carl-lentz-hesitates-to-call-himself-evangelical-says -term-has-been-hijacked.html.

26   *Jesus would not*: DeRay McKesson, "Transformational Leadership: DeRay McKesson," Yale Divinity School, YouTube, October 11, 2016, https://youtu.be /WlFIuVA5GXs.

All Lives Matter: Rachel Hoover, "Rev. Graham Blasts 'All Lives Matter' Suspension, Says 'Free Speech Is Under Attack' and 'Every Life Matters,'" cnsnews.com, August 11, 2016, www.cnsnews.com/blog/rachel-hoover/rev-graham-blasts-all -lives-matter-suspension-says-free-speech-under-attack-and.

27   *I don't mean to be insensitive*: Roy S. Johnson, "Gardendale Pastor's 'Get On a Boat' Apology Sinks In Sea of Ignorance," al.com, October 3, 2017, updated January 13, 2019, www.al.com/opinion/2017/10/gardendale_pastors_get_on_a_bo.html.

28   *When Lecrae went public*: Carol Kuruvilla, "Rapper Has Choice Words for Christians Who Don't Want Him to Talk About Race," *HuffPost*, July 12, 2016, www .huffpost.com/entry-lecrae-rapper-christian-black-lives-matter_n_5783ff28e4b034 4d51508a2e.

Dove Awards edited: The Crew, "Kirk Franklin Will Not Attend Dove Awards or Anything Associated with TBN Due to Speech Being Cut," YouTube, accessed December 17, 2019 https://youtu.be/_ZBioFNQUrQ.

30   *The same report shows*: "Millennials: Confident. Connected. Open to Change," Social & Demographic Trends, Pew Research Center, February 24, 2010, www.pew socialtrends.org/2010/02/24/millennials-confident-connected-open-to-change.

31 *[Young people] want*: Caroline Newman, "Why Millennials Are Leaving Religion but Embracing Spirituality," *UVA Today*, December 14, 2015, https://news.virginia.edu/content/qa-why-millennials-are-leaving-religion-embracing-spirituality.

32 *I believe*: Robert Morris, "A Lack of Understanding," Gatewaychurchtv, October 21, 2017, YouTube, https://youtu.be/kcNXWpk7Pbw.

Jesus loves the little children: "Jesus Loves the Little Children," lyrics by C. Herbert Woolston, music by George F. Root, 1864 (music originally written for American Civil War song "Tramp, Tramp, Tramp").

3. THE QUEST FOR THE SOULS

34 *the only white people*: Adam Yuster, "Emmys: Read Michael Che and Colin Jost's Opening Monologue," *The Hollywood Reporter*, September 17, 2018, www.hollywoodreporter.com/news/michael-che-colin-jost-s-2018-emmys-opening-monologue-1144710.

The church must be reminded: Martin Luther King Jr., "A Knock at Midnight," The Martin Luther King Jr. Research Education Institute at Stanford University, June 11, 1967, https://kinginstitute.stanford.edu/king-papers/documents/knock-midnight.

36 *The greatest hindrance*: *Trigger Warning with Killer Mike*, episode 4, "New Jesus," directed by Vikram Gandhi, aired 2019, on Netflix.

37 *Jesus of Lubeck*: "Adventurers and Slavers," The National Archives, accessed December 6, 2019, www.nationalarchives.gov.uk/pathways/blackhistory/early_times/adventurers.htm.

38 *It isn't a religion*: Jacob Dorman, *Chosen People: The Rise of American Black Israelite Religions* (Oxford: Oxford University Press, 2013), 4.

39 *prominent hip-hop artist Kendrick Lamar*: Grant Shreve, "Kendrick Lamar and Black Israelism," *JSTOR Daily*, May 7, 2018, https://daily.jstor.org/kendrick-lamar-and-black-israelism.

on the street corners: Shreve, "Kendrick Lamar."

41 *They claim to teach*: "About Us," Israelite School of Universal Practical Knowledge, accessed December 6, 2019, https://isupk.com/about-us.

the SPLC reports: "Racist Black Hebrew Israelites Becoming More Militant," Intelligence Report, Southern Poverty Law Center, August 29, 2008, www.splcenter.org/fighting-hate/intelligence-report/2008/racist-black-hebrew-israelites-becoming-more-militant.

43 *Wallace D. Fard Muhammad, the founder*: Tasneem Paghdiwala, "The Aging of the Moors," *Chicago Reader*, November 15, 2007, www.chicagoreader.com/chicago/the-aging-of-the-moors/Content?oid=999633.

44 *The NOI claims*: Tynetta Muhammad, "Brief History on Origin of the Nation of Islam," Nation of Islam, March 28, 1996, www.noi.org/noi-history.

One did not need: James Baldwin, "The Fire Next Time," in *Baldwin: Collected Essays*, ed. Toni Morrison (New York: Library Classics of the United States, 1998), 315.

the natural religions: Malcolm X, *The Autobiography of Malcolm X* (New York: Random House Group, 2015), 179.

46 *W. E. B. Du Bois famously said*: W. E. B. Du Bois, *The Souls of Black Folk* (New York: Bantam Books, 1903), 5.

47   *The negro church of today*: Du Bois, *Souls of Black Folk*, 136.
     This building: Du Bois, *Souls of Black Folk*, 136.

4. THE CHURCH AND THE SEARCH FOR IDENTITY

50   *Black males are nearly*: Alan Neuhauser, "Black Males 3 Times More Likely to Be
     Killed by Police," *US News & World Report*, December 21, 2016, www.usnews
     .com/news/national-news/articles/2016-12-21/black-males-nearly-3-times-more
     -likely-to-be-killed-by-police-than-whites.

     Black students, particularly boys: Tom Loveless, "2017 Brown Center Report on
     American Education: Race and School Suspensions," Brookings, March 22, 2017,
     www.brookings.edu/research/2017-brown-center-report-part-iii-race-and-school
     -suspensions.

     Additionally, research reveals: Michael A. Lindsey, Ariell H. Sheftall, Yunyu Xiao, and
     Sean Joe, "Trends of Suicidal Behaviors Among High School Students in the United
     States: 19912017," *Pediatrics*, November 2019, https://pediatrics.aappublications
     .org/content/144/5/e20191187.

     the rate of suicide attempts: Lindsey et al., "Trends of Suicidal Behaviors."

     Another study reveals: Inger E. Burnett-Zeigler, "Young Black People Are Killing
     Themselves: The Numbers Are Shocking," *New York Times*, December 16, 2019,
     www.nytimes.com/2019/12/16/opinion/young-black-people-suicide.html.

55   *A few years ago*: Aisha Harris, "Santa Claus Should Not Be a White Man Anymore,"
     Slate, December 10, 2013, https://slate.com/human-interest/2013/12/santa-claus
     -an-old-white-man-not-anymore-meet-santa-the-penguin-a-new-christmas
     -symbol.html.

     Get over it: Megyn Kelly, "Kelly: Jesus Was a White Man Too," CNN, December 13,
     2013, www.cnn.com/videos/bestoftv/2013/12/13/sot-megyn-kelly-santa-is-white.cnn.

56   *The United States is 4.4 percent*: Roy Walmsley, "World Prison Population List"
     (tenth edition), International Centre for Prison Studies, November 21, 2013, www
     .prisonstudies.org/sites/default/files/resources/downloads/wppl_10.pdf.

59   *For example, evangelical Christians missed*: Aric Jenkins, "Read President Trump's
     NFL Speech on National Anthem Protests," *Time*, September 23, 2017, https://time
     .com/4954684/donald-trump-nfl-speech-anthem-protests.

     Keep the political comments: Emily Sullivan, "Laura Ingraham Told LeBron James to
     Shut Up and Dribble; He Went to the Hoop," NPR, February 19, 2018, www.npr
     .org/sections/thetwo-way/2018/02/19/587097707/laura-ingraham-told-lebron
     -james-to-shutup-and-dribble-he-went-to-the-hoop.

61   *identity crisis cycles*: Susan Krauss Whitbourne, "Are You Having an Identity Crisis? 4
     Key Ways to Identify Your Identity," *Psychology Today*, March 3, 2012, www.psychology
     today.com/us/blog/fulfillment-any-age/201203/are-you-having-identity-crisis.

     39 percent of jail inmates: "Statistics," The Fatherless Generation, US Department
     of Justice 2002 Survey of 7,000 Inmates, accessed January 9, 2020, https://thefather
     lessgeneration.wordpress.com/statistics.

5. THE CHRISTIAN'S SCANDALOUS THINKING

68   *Instead of immediately rejecting*: Brian K. Blount, *Can I Get a Witness?: Reading Revelation Through African American Culture* (Louisville, KY: Westminster John Knox, 2005), 6.

Everything else is thought: Cain Hope Felder, ed., *Stony the Road We Trod: African American Biblical Interpretation* (Minneapolis, MN: Augsburg Fortress, 1991), 6.

69   *What passes for normative hermeneutics*: Felder, *Stony the Road We Trod*, 6.

70   *[Those who train ministers]*: William H. Myers, "The Hermeneutical Dilemma of the African American Biblical Student," in *Stony the Road We Trod: African American Biblical Interpretation*, ed. Cain Hope Felder (Minneapolis, MN: Augsburg Fortress, 1991), 40.

71   *Between the Christianity of this land*: Samuel Brooke, *Slavery, and the Slaveholder's Religion: As Opposed to Christianity* (Cincinnati, OH: printed by the author, 1846), 70.

72   *Traditional theological education*: John Barton, *The Nature of Biblical Criticism* (Louisville, KY: Westminster John Knox, 2007).

77   *a new nation could be formed*: Vincent L. Wimbush, "The Bible and African Americans: An Outline of an Interpretive History," in *Stony the Road We Trod: African American Biblical Interpretation*, ed. Cain Hope Felder (Minneapolis, MN: Augsburg Fortress, 1991), 110.

78   *certain reading[s] of the Abrahamic myth*: Wimbush, "The Bible and African Americans," 111.

should not be interpreted arbitrarily: Brian K. Blount, *Cultural Interpretation: Reorienting New Testament Criticism* (Minneapolis, MN: Augsburg Fortress, 1995), 3.

Eurocentric standard: Blount, *Cultural Interpretation*, 3.

79   *Attorney General Jeff Sessions*: Julie Zauzmer and Keith McMillan, "Sessions Cites Bible Passage Used to Defend Slavery in Defense of Separating Immigrant Families," *Washington Post*, June 15, 2018, www.washingtonpost.com/news/acts-of-faith /wp/2018/06/14/jeff-sessions-points-to-the-bible-in-defense-of-separating-immi grant-families.

80   *When multiple voices*: Blount, *Cultural Interpretation*, 3.

We need more people of color: Myers, "The Hermeneutical Dilemma," 49-50.

6. THE COLOR OF THE BIBLE

82   *Biblical characters lived*: Paul Harvey, "'A Servant of Servants Shall He Be': The Construction of Race in American Religious Mythologies," in *Religion and the Creation of Race and Ethnicity: An Introduction*, ed. Craig R. Prentiss (New York: New York University Press, 2003), 13-27.

84   *The Bible tells us repeatedly*: The following are examples of moments that explicitly show the Lord looks kindly on those who welcome different ethnicities into their homes: Gen 12:1-3; 12:10-20; 15:13; 18:2-5; 20:15; 26:11; 23:3-6; 37:1; 41:38-43; Ex 1:8-10, 15-21; 12:49; 22:20; 23:9; Lev 19:10, 33-34; 25:23; Num 15:14-16; 20:14-21; 23:9; Deut 10:16-19; 24:14, 17, 19-21; 26:5, 11; 27:19; 1 Kings 8:41-43; Ps 39:13; 146:9; Is 1:17; 10:1; 11:6; 16:3-4; 56:8; 66:18; Jer 7:6-7; 22:3; Ezek 16:3; 22:6-7; 22:29-30; 47:21-23; Mal 3:5.

Cut Africa out of the Bible: Thomas C. Oden, *How Africa Shaped the Christian Mind: Rediscovering the African Seedbed in Western Christianity* (Downers Grove, IL: InterVarsity Press, 2007), 14.

85   *depraved, excessive, contagious*: John Dominic Crossan, *The Birth of Christianity* (Edinburgh: T&T Clark, 1999), 3-19.

      But others relentlessly held: "Letters of Pliny the Younger and the Emperor Trajan," *PBS: Frontline*, translated by William Whiston, accessed January 4, 2020, www.pbs .org/wgbh/pages/frontline/shows/religion/maps/primary/pliny.html.

      This positiveness and inflexibile obstinacy: "Letters of Pliny," *PBS: Frontline*.

88   *Particularly, slaveholders deployed images*: See Edward Blum and Paul Harvey, *The Color of Christ* (Chapel Hill: The University of North Carolina Press, 2012), 160-83.

89   *Whether through tracts*: Blum and Harvey, *The Color of Christ*, 15.

90   *the image of Jesus*: Blum and Harvey, *The Color of Christ*, 287.

      You know, of course: Upton Sinclair, *They Call Me Carpenter: A Tale of the Second Coming* (Scotts Valley, CA: CreateSpace Publishing, 2013), 5.

91   *propaganda films*: Sinclair, *They Call Me Carpenter*, 5. Also, see Blum and Harvey, *The Color of Christ*, 259.

92   *God and biblical figures*: Anthony Pinn, *The African American Religious Experience* (London: Greenwood Press, 2006), 78.

93   *All the pictures I've seen*: Blum and Harvey, *The Color of Christ*, 304.

      Hollywood films about Jesus: Catherine Jones and Atsushi Tajima, "The Caucasian-ization of Jesus: Hollywood Transforming Christianity into a Racially Hierarchical Discourse," *Journal of Religion and Popular Culture* 27, no. 3 (Fall 2015): 202-19.

7. THE GENESIS CURSE?

95   *angels as Scandinavian*: Keith August Burton, *The Blessing of Africa* (Downers Grove, IL: IVP Academic, 2007), 11.

98   *Alexandria near Egypt*: Robert Hood, *Begrimed and Black: Christian Traditions on Black and Blackness* (Minneapolis, MN: Fortress Press, 1994), 59.

      where the faith: Hood, *Begrimed and Black*, 112.

      The ancient Greeks and Romans: Hood, *Begrimed and Black*, 59.

99   *The smallest infusion*: Hood, *Begrimed and Black*, 159.

      catchall term: Hood, *Begrimed and Black*, 159.

      The so-called Portuguese Empire: "Portuguese Empire," New World Encyclopedia, ac-cessed October 21, 2019, www.newworldencyclopedia.org/entry/Portuguese_Empire.

100   *Along the east coast*: "History of the Portuguese Empire," HistoryWorld, accessed Oc-tober 21, 2019, www.historyworld.net/wrldhis/PlainTextHistories.asp?historyid=ab48.

101   *The myth has become*: Burton, *The Blessing of Africa*, 11.

102   *The formation of American culture*: Burton, *The Blessing of Africa*, 179.

      Ham is Hebrew for: Burton, *The Blessing of Africa*, 23.

103   *Japheth alone received Christianity*: Burton, *The Blessing of Africa*, 23. See also Hood, *Begrimed and Black*, 157.

      The declaration of: Burton, *The Blessing of Africa*, 160.

      Where, then, I ask: Burton, *The Blessing of Africa*, 160.

103 *The Ham legend*: Burton, *The Blessing of Africa*, 70.

104 *The kingdoms of Kush*: Burton, *The Blessing of Africa*, 26.

According to the Table of Nations: Burton, *The Blessing of Africa*, 27.

105 *However, Canaan's territory*: Burton, *The Blessing of Africa*, 28.

Ethiopia has been: Hood, *Begrimed and Black*, 59.

However, the same kings: Hood, *Begrimed and Black*, 158.

8. READING THE NEW TESTAMENT THROUGH DARK LENSES

110 *How can she say*: Crystal Valentine, "And the News Reporter Says Jesus Is White," Button Poetry, April 21, 2016, YouTube, www.youtube.com/watch?v=bPEdcr_XePk.

Killer Mike argues: *Trigger Warning with Killer Mike*, episode 4, "New Jesus," directed by Vikram Gandhi, aired 2019, on Netflix.

113 *I believe that until*: James H. Cone, "James Cone: 'The Cross and the Lynching Tree,'" Vanderbilt University, April 5, 2013, YouTube, www.youtube.com/watch?v=htj59Cup7Jg.

114 *God descends to humanity*: Jacques Ellul, *Perspectives on Our Age: Jacques Ellul Speaks on His Life and Work*, ed. Willem H. Vanderburg (Toronto: House of Anansi, 2004), 78.

In the midst: Martin Luther King Jr., "Letter from Birmingham Jail," 1963, http://web.cn.edu/kwheeler/documents/letter_birmingham_jail.pdf.

116 *Research reveals that prospective employers*: Lincoln Quillian, Devah Pager, Ole Hexel, and Arnfinn H. Midtboen, "Meta-Analysis of Field Experiments Shows No Change in Racial Discrimination in Hiring Over Time," *Proceedings of the National Academy of Sciences of the United States of America*, September 12, 2017, www.pnas.org/content/early/2017/09/11/1706255114.

121 *Cheap grace is the preaching of forgiveness*: Dietrich Bonhoeffer, *The Cost of Discipleship*, trans. R. H. Fuller, rev. ed. (New York: Macmillan, 1960), 36.

9. SOCIAL JUSTICE AND THE BIBLE

123 *For instance, a group of evangelical pastors*: "The Statement on Social Justice and the Gospel," https://statementonsocialjustice.com, accessed September 12, 2019.

124 *The Italian Roman Catholic Jesuit*: Antipas L. Harris and Michael D. Palmer, *The Holy Spirit and Social Justice: Interdisciplinary Global Perspectives*, History, Race, and Culture (Lanham, MD: Seymour Press, 2019), 2.

Social justice is: Harris and Palmer, *The Holy Spirit and Social Justice*, xvii.

125 *The task of prophetic imagination*: Walter Brueggemann, *The Prophetic Imagination*, 2nd ed. (Minneapolis, MN: Fortress Press, 2001), 65.

hold the Bible: The exact quote "We must hold the Bible in one hand and the newspaper in the other" is in fact an interpretation of things he said in interviews during the 1960s. According to the Center for Barth Studies at Princeton Theological Seminary, they have found no direct and authoritative source. For more details, visit barth.ptsem.edu/about-cbs/faq.

127 *And as we walk*: Martin Luther King Jr., "Chapter 20: March on Washington," The Martin Luther King Jr. Research Education Institute at Stanford University, accessed December 7, 2019, https://kinginstitute.stanford.edu/chapter-20-march-washington.

128   *While efforts*: William Wilberforce, *An Appeal to the Religion, Justice, and Humanity of the Inhabitants of the British Empire: On Behalf of the Negro Slaves in the West Indies* (London: J. Hatchard and Son, 1823), 75.

129   *And the way to solve*: Martin Luther King Jr., "Conquering Self-Centeredness: Sermon delivered at Dexter Avenue Baptist Church," The Martin Luther King Jr. Research Education Institute at Stanford University, accessed December 7, 2019, https://king institute.stanford.edu/king-papers/documents/conquering-self-centeredness -sermon-delivered-dexter-avenue-baptist-church.

10. A NEW WAY TO THINK ABOUT THE FAITH

149   *Returning hate for hate*: Martin Luther King Jr., *A Gift of Love: Sermons from Strength to Love and Other Preaching* (Boston: Beacon Press, 1963), 49.

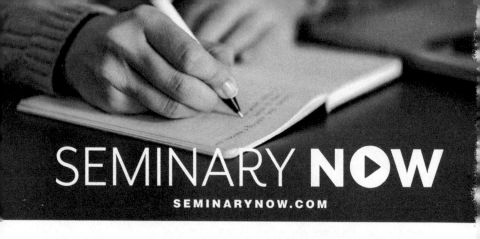

SEMINARY NOW

SEMINARYNOW.COM

UNIQUE CONTENT AND DIVERSE VOICES FOR MINISTRY TODAY

A COMPANION VIDEO COURSE taught by the author of this book is available on the Seminary Now platform. Visit seminarynow.com to access this course and many others.

IVP partners with Seminary Now to produce video courses on select titles. Seminary Now is a subscription-based educational platform providing video courses on topics that help prepare ministry leaders for today's challenges.

SEMINARY NOW COURSES COVER TOPICS IN THE FOLLOWING AREAS:
- Biblical and Theological Foundations
- Old and New Testament Studies
- Church and Mission
- Ministry
- Justice and Reconciliation

AND EACH COURSE FEATURES CONTENT THAT IS:
- Accessible on most mobile, desktop, and smart TV devices
- Presented in short, 12-15 minute segments
- Offered in conjunction with a course study guide and assessment

To see the current course offerings or for more information on how to subscribe to the platform, visit seminarynow.com.

 **InterVarsity Press**
ivpress.com